The eschatological is an older s
teric (Geerhardus Vos). *Last Th*
fundamental for a sound over
with valuable insights of its own. with an extensive awareness
of and reference to relevant literature, it addresses in a stimu-
lating fashion issues that bear on such basic biblical themes
as God's purposes in creation, the relationship between creation and redemption, and the work of Christ. While there is
room to disagree at points, anyone interested in the biblical
basis for covenant theology will read Fesko with great profit.

Richard Gaffin,
Westminster Theological Seminary, Philadelphia

If beginnings are crucial for understanding the essence of
something in the ancient Near East, which they are, then
thankfully John Fesko has shown us how integrated and
important protology is for our reading of Scripture and our
theological constructions. In a work that is thoroughly covenantal, Fesko sets forth a well-reasoned argument to demonstrate that the patterns, themes, and imagery of protology
keep reappearing in Scripture and those patterns have a defi-
nite eschatological goal: Christ our Lord is the penalty payer
and probation keeper.

Bryan D. Estelle,
Westminster Seminary, California

Many people would affirm the importance of the opening
chapters of Genesis, but not all of them for the right reasons.
John Fesko's work has the great virtue of considering not only
many of the common controversial issues associated with
Genesis 1–3, but also issues of equal and greater importance
that are too often undervalued, such as the image of God,
the covenant with Adam, and the way that the early chapters
of Scripture point us to Christ and his redemptive work.
Dr. Fesko takes his readers through much detailed, careful
exegetical study while constantly reflecting on the broader
theological ramifications of these fundamental biblical texts.
The final result is a book that should stimulate reflection on
a host of crucial matters, re-focus our impoverished views of
Genesis 1–3, and reinforce the truth that Christ is the center
of the Scriptures.

David VanDrunen,
Westminster Seminary, California

So much literature on Genesis 1 to 3 is concerned either with its relationship to science or else with its relevance for the male/female issue. This volume is refreshingly different and should be warmly welcomed, for Dr. Fesko leads us along a quite different path by interpreting these chapters in terms of Christ and the final consummation of God's purposes in him. There is so much here to stimulate the Christian reader and to move us towards a more Christocentric view of God's purpose for his universe.

Geoffrey Grogan,
International Christian College, Glasgow, Scotland

Last Things First

Unlocking Genesis 1–3 with
the Christ of Eschatology

J. V. Fesko

MENTOR

Copyright © J. V. Fesko 2007

ISBN 1-84550-229-9
ISBN 978-1-84550-229-4

10 9 8 7 6 5 4 3 2 1

Published in 2007
in the
Mentor Imprint
by
Christian Focus Publications,
Geanies House, Fearn, Ross-shire,
IV20 1TW, Scotland, UK

www.christianfocus.com

Cover design by moose77.com

Printed and bound by Bell & Bain, Glasgow

CONTENTS

To Anneke, Wife

עֶצֶם מֵעֲצָמַי וּבָשָׂר מִבְּשָׂרִי

ABBREVIATIONS

AB	Anchor Bible
ACCS	Ancient Christian Commentary on Scripture
ANE	ancient Near East
ANE 2	*The Ancient Near East (Volume II): A New Anthology of Texts and Pictures* ed. J. B. Pritchard
ANF	Ante-Nicene Fathers
BDB	Brown, Driver and Briggs Hebrew Lexicon
BECNT	Baker Exegetical Commentary on the New Testament
BNTC	Black's New Testament Commentary
BibSac	*Bibliotheca Sacra*
CBQ	*Catholic Biblical Quarterly*
CNTC	*Calvin New Testament Commentary*
CTJ	*Calvin Theological Journal*
CTS	Calvin Translation Society
EBC	Expositor's Bible Commentary
ESV	English Standard Version
ICC	International Critical Commentary
JBL	*Journal of Biblical Literature*
JETS	*Journal of the Evangelical Theological Society*
JPSTC	Jewish Publication Society Torah Commentary
KJV	King James Version
LCC	Library of Christian Classics
LW	Luther's Works
LXX	Septuagint (Greek translation of Old Testament)
Mid. Rabb.	*Midrash Rabbah*
MT	Masoretic Text

NASV	New American Standard Version
NCBC	New Cambridge Bible Commentary
NIB	New Interpreter's Bible
NICNT	New International Commentary on the New Testament
NICOT	New International Commentary on the Old Testament
NIDNTT	New International Dictionary of New Testament Theology
NIDOTTE	New International Dictionary of Old Testament Theology and Exegesis
NIGTC	New International Greek Testament Commentary
NIV	New International Version
NIVAC	NIV Application Commentary
NKJV	New King James Version
NLT	New Living Translation
NPNF	Nicene and Post-Nicene Fathers
NRSV	New Revised Standard Version
NSBT	New Studies in Biblical Theology
NT	Novum Testamentum
NTC	New Testament Commentary
OTL	Old Testament Library
PTR	*Princeton Theological Review*
TOTC	*Tyndale Old Testament Commentary*
VT	*Vetus Testamentum*
Vul.	*Vulgate (Latin translation of Bible)*
WBC	*Word Biblical Commentary*
WTJ	*Westminster Theological Journal*
ZAW	*Zeitschrift für die alttestamentliche Wissenschaft*

PREFACE

This book began life as a series of Sunday School lectures for the adults in my church. At the time, there were significant debates surrounding the length of the days of creation in the Reformed community and I thought that a study on Genesis 1–3 would be helpful for the congregation.

In my lecture preparation I continually found myself turning back and forth between the books of Genesis and Revelation in an effort to understand what was occurring in the seemingly straightforward but nonetheless mysterious first three chapters of the Bible. The more I studied these chapters the more I realized the importance of interpreting them as the New Testament authors did – with a view to Christ and eschatology. In other words, – why is Christ called the 'last Adam'? That he is the 'last' is most assuredly connected with the end, with eschatology, and that he is called 'Adam' ties Jesus to the first man. I would soon tell my Sunday School class and later my RTS students that Genesis 1–3 is the most familiar but ironically unfamiliar terrain in all of Scripture.

Many come to the chapters thinking they know what occurs therein – creation, man, fall – and they then move along never realizing that they have entered the shadowlands, the land of the types of Christ and his work. This book represents my efforts to explain Genesis 1–3 in the light of Christ and eschatology.

Hopefully this book, which is ultimately a work of biblical theology, will be a contribution towards demonstrating that, as Geerhardus Vos once wrote, 'Dogmatics is the crown which grows out of all the work that Biblical Theology can accomplish.' Hopefully this book will help to 'demonstrate that the fundamental doctrines of our faith do not rest, as many would fain believe, on an arbitrary exposition of some isolated proof-texts. It will not so much prove these doctrines, as it will do what is far better than proof – make them grow out organically before our eyes from the stem of revelation.'[1] In other words, the case made in this book will demonstrate the validity of the systematic theological constructs of the covenants of works and grace, a common staple of historic Reformed dogmatics. To this end, this book is not intended as a replacement for but an aid to systematic theology, to be read in tandem with a theological work like that of Louis Berkhof.[2] Contrary to recent trends, biblical studies is not antithetical to systematic theology.

Books are never written in a vacuum, and to that end I have many people to thank for their assistance in seeing its publication. I want to thank many friends and colleagues who read early drafts of portions of this book and provided helpful comments: John Muether, Bill Dennison, and Samuel Bray. I also want to thank those who were willing to allow me to bludgeon them with the entire manuscript and who provided me with helpful comments and interaction: Bryan Estelle, Dick Gaffin, Wally King, and Dave VanDrunen. I am also grateful to the adult Sunday School class at Geneva OPC for their attentiveness over nine months of Sunday mornings going through this material, to my RTS-Atlanta hermeneutics class in the Spring of 2004 and several

---

[1]Geerhardus Vos, 'The Idea of Biblical Theology as a Science and as a Theological Discipline,' in Richard B. Gaffin, Jr., ed., *Redemptive History and Biblical Interpretation: The Shorter Writings of Geerhardus Vos* (Phillipsburg: P & R, 1980), p. 24.

[2]Louis Berkhof, *Systematic Theology: New Combined Edition* (1932-38; Grand Rapids: Eerdmans, 1996).

classes of systematics students. I want to thank my session, Wally King and Bud Winslow, both for their encouragement to pursue the project and for the church's financial support through a generous book allowance. Geneva's generosity saved me countless hours of sitting in Atlanta traffic where I could instead research in the quiet confines of my study and mark up the books that I had purchased. I want to thank Malcolm Maclean, my editor, and the editorial staff at Christian Focus for all of their hard work in getting this book to press. None of these people deserve the blame for any of the deficiencies in this book; the credit for any deficiency belongs to me alone. Their help, nevertheless, is greatly appreciated.

This book was originally titled *Protology*, but my wife thought it sounded too much like 'proctology', and my editor also thought it was too technical. I therefore enlisted the help of my mother-in-law, Linda Jones, who surveyed Sunday lunch-time guests for ideas and was able to come up with the much better title of, *Last Things First*, from WTS student Jason Kirklin. So, I owe thanks to my mother-in-law for that valiant effort in rescuing my book from an obscure and boring title! I would also like to thank my parents and my brother and his wife for their love, prayers, and support. I would like to thank my wife, Anneke, for helping me socialize many of the ideas in the book and who is a constant source of encouragement, love, and much joy. It is to you, wife, that I dedicate this book. I pray that this book edifies the church, the bride of Christ, and brings glory to the eschatological Adam, Jesus Christ. *Soli Deo Gloria.*

INTRODUCTION

Genesis has long drawn the attention of students of the Scriptures and has held nearly universal esteem within the Church. Despite this esteem, the book's opening chapters have challenged interpreters throughout the ages. Martin Luther once wrote that 'the first chapter is written in the simplest language; yet it contains matters of the utmost importance and very difficult to understand. It was for this reason, as St. Jerome asserts, that among the Hebrews it was forbidden for anyone under thirty to read the chapter or to expound it for others.'[1] While the matters in Genesis 1–3 appear to be written rather simply, varying opinion regarding its interpretation certainly supports Luther's claim.

Over the past several centuries some have argued that the great age of the earth is compatible with Genesis, and others claim that it is only several thousand years old. Some have taught that Genesis fits evolutionary theory and others that it contradicts it. More recently, especially in the Reformed community, debate has swirled around the issue of the length of the days

---

[1]Martin Luther, *Lectures on Genesis*, LW, vol. 1, ed. Jaroslav Pelikan (St. Louis: Concordia, 1958), p. 3.

[2]On this debate, see David Hagopian, ed, *The Genesis Debate: Three Views on the Days of Creation* (Mission Viejo: Crux Press, 2001); James B. Jordan, *Creation in Six Days: A Defense of the Traditional Reading of Genesis One* (Moscow: Canon, 1999); Kenneth L. Gentry and Michael R. Butler, *Yea, Hath God Said?: The Framework Hypothesis/Six-Day Creation Debate* (Eugene: Wipf & Stock, 2002); Douglas F. Kelly, *Creation and Change: Genesis 1.1-2.4 in the Light of Changing Scientific Paradigms* (Fearn: Mentor, 1997); Joseph A. Pipa,

of creation.[2] There are many debates and various theologians who represent different schools of thought. Is there a better way to approach the opening chapters of Genesis in spite of the debate? The answer to this question is an unqualified, Yes. The answer comes neither through the length of the days nor in using the canons of science to interpret Genesis. The way through the impasse is to interpret Genesis in the manner presented in the New Testament. More specifically, one must interpret Genesis 1–3 in the light of Christ and eschatology. Therefore, we should first examine current popular approaches to the inter-pretation of Genesis 1–3 and see their deficiencies in order to see the necessity for a christological and eschatological interpretation.

Popular approaches to Genesis

In the past two centuries debate over Genesis has largely centered upon science, particularly the evolutionary theories of Charles Darwin.[3] Christians, in one way or another, have sought to use the Scriptures as a bulwark against Darwin's theories regarding the origins of man. Various schools of thought have responded to evolutionary theory by developing different interpretations of Genesis 1–3.

Old Princeton: Warfield and Hodge

One of the best-known responses to evolutionary theory came from the Old School Presbyterianism of Princeton Seminary in the nineteenth century. B. B. Warfield believed that evolutionary theory and Genesis 1–3 were in harmony. Concerning John Calvin's doctrine of creation, Warfield writes:

Jr. and David W. Hall, eds, *Did God Create in Six Days?* (Greenville: Southern Presbyterian Press, 1999); E. J. Young, *Studies in Genesis One* (Phillipsburg: P & R, n. d.).

[3]See Charles Darwin, *The Origin of Species* (1859; New York: Modern Library, 1998); *idem, The Voyage of the Beagle* (1839; New Yok: Modern Library, 2001).

It should be scarcely passed without remark that Calvin's doctrine of creation is, if we have understood it aright, for all except the souls of men, an evolutionary one. The 'ingested mass,' including the 'promise and potency' of all that was yet to be, was called into being by the simple *fiat* of God. But all that has come into being since – except the souls of men alone – has arisen as a modification of this original world-stuff by means of the interaction of its intrinsic forces. Not these forces apart from God, of course ... but in the sense that all the modifications of the world-stuff have taken place under the directly upholding and governing hand of God, and find their account ultimately in His will. But they find their account proximately in 'second causes'; and this is not only evolutionism but pure evolutionism.[4]

Warfield believed that God created everything *ex nihilo* by divine fiat, i.e. 'Let there be light' (Gen. 1:3). After the initial creation by God, everything else, including man's body, developed in an evolutionary fashion.[5] God started it all and then secondary evolutionary causes took over, excepting God's direct creation of the soul of man. How did Warfield harmonize Scripture with evolutionary theory? He did so in the same manner as his predecessor, Charles Hodge.

Hodge argued that Genesis, when it says that the creation was completed in six days, conflicts with the evidence of geology, which says that the earth is much older. He writes that

[4]B. B. Warfield, 'Calvin's Doctrine of the Creation,' in *Works*, vol. 5, ed. E. D. Warfield (Grand Rapids: Baker, 1981), pp. 304-05.

[5]B. B. Warfield, 'Review of James Orr, *God's Image in Man and Its Defacement in the Light of Modern Denials*,' in Mark A. Noll and David N. Livingstone, eds, *B. B. Warfield: Evolution, Science, and Scripture: Selected Writings* (Grand Rapids: Baker, 2000), p. 233; also idem, *PTR* 4 (1906), pp. 455-58.

it is of course admitted that, taking this account by itself, it would be most natural to understand the word ['day'] in its ordinary sense; but if that sense brings the Mosaic account into conflict with facts, and another sense avoids such conflict, then it is obligatory on us to adopt the other. Now it is urged that if the word 'day' be taken in the sense of 'an indefinite period of time,' a sense which it undoubtedly has in other parts of Scripture, there is not only no discrepancy between the Mosaic account of the creation and the assumed facts of geology, but there is a more marvelous coincidence between them.[6]

Hodge's methodology is clear: geology informs his interpretation of the opening chapters of Genesis. In this manner Hodge and Warfield harmonize Genesis 1–3 with evolutionary theory. Creation takes place, not in six 24-hour days, but in six undefined periods of time. Though not agreeing at every point, Hugh Ross has most recently employed this type of exegesis of Genesis 1–3.[7] Others have interacted with Genesis and science much differently than Hodge and Warfield.

Creation science: Henry Morris
If one characterizes the Old Princeton position as accommodating Genesis to science, he may say the inverse regarding Creation science. Creation science adherents accommodate science to their interpretation of Scripture.

Henry Morris lists first among the teachings of Genesis that it tells of the origins of the universe. Morris writes that 'Genesis stands alone in accounting for the actual creation of the basic space-mass-time continuum which constitutes our physical universe'.[8] With this

---

[6]Charles Hodge, *Systematic Theology*, 3 vols. (1889; Grand Rapids: Eerdmans, 1991), vol. 1, pp. 570-71.

[7]See Hugh Ross & Gleason L. Archer, 'The Day-Age View,' in *The Genesis Debate: Three Views on the Days of Creation*, ed. David G. Hagopian (Mission Viejo: Crux Press, 2001), pp. 123-64.

presupposition and a literalistic hermeneutic in hand, Morris concludes that 'the only proper way to interpret Genesis 1 is not to "interpret" it at all. That is, we accept the fact that it was meant to say exactly what it says. The "days" are literal days and the events described happened in just the way described.'[9] Genesis, according to Morris' interpretation, teaches that God created the cosmos in six 24-hour periods.

What about scientific evidence that suggests the cosmos is much older? This is where theologians accommodate science to their interpretation of Scripture.

One creation science proponent, Douglas Kelly, argues that scientific theory and the Genesis account conflict regarding the age of the universe because scientists consider the speed of light to be an unchanging constant. Scientists know that light travels at approximately 186,000 miles per second and can therefore calculate the time light from the nearest star takes to reach earth. This is how scientists conclude that the cosmos is millions of years old. If the nearest star, other than the sun, is 4.22 light-years away, then the cosmos must be at least this old. The distance to the furthest star, however, is some 18 billion light-years away. Kelly resolves this conflict by arguing that the speed of light is not constant. He states that 'the speed of light in 1675 was 2.6% higher than today'. In other words, if light traveled 2.6% faster just several hundred years ago, then it must have traveled much faster thousands of years ago. Thus, the cosmos is not as old as most scientists think.[10] Kelly and Morris reject current scientific claims and modify scientific theory to conform to their interpretation of Scripture. Creation

---

[8]Henry Morris, *The Genesis Record: A Scientific & Devotional Commentary on the Book of Beginnings* (Grand Rapids: Baker, 1976), p. 18.

[9]Morris, *Genesis Record*, p. 54.

[10]Kelly, *Creation and Change (Christian Focus Publications, 1997)*, pp. 144ff.

science has had a great deal of influence in recent years, even in the Reformed community. What makes this observation interesting is that the creation science movement grows out of theological and hermeneutical presuppositions antithetical to Reformed theology. How does creation science conflict with Reformed theology?

Presuppositions of the two popular approaches

Creation science
Since the advent of the presuppositional apologetics of Cornelius Van Til, several generations of Reformed theologians and ministers have learned to question presuppositions. In this regard Van Til writes,

> We ought to find small comfort in the idea that others too, for example, non-Christian scientists, have to make assumptions... We all make assumptions, but we alone do not make false assumptions. The fact that all make assumptions is in itself a mere psychological and formal matter. The question is as to who makes the right assumptions or presuppositions.[11]

Yet many within the Reformed community accept the conclusions of creation science without investigating its presuppositions. To find the presuppositions of creation science one must examine its history. The founder of the creation science movement was George McCready Price (1870–1963), a Seventh-Day Adventist and self-taught geologist. He was the only individual William Jennings Bryan cited in the Scopes trial as an anti-evolution scientist. The second generation of creation scientists came in the 1960s with the work of Henry Morris and the publication of *The Genesis Flood*, which he wrote with John Whitcomb. Few note, however, that Morris and Whitcomb are dispensationalists.[12] Whitcomb

---

[11]Cornelius Van Til, *Common Grace and the Gospel* (Phillipsburg: P & R, 1972), p. 50.

was a professor of theology at Grace Theological Seminary, a dispensationalist institution. What marks dispensationalism?

The hallmark hermeneutical principle of dispensationalism is strict literalism. Charles Ryrie writes that, 'If plain or normal interpretation is the only valid hermeneutical principle, and if it is consistently applied, it will cause one to be a dispensationalist. As basic as one believes normal interpretation to be, to that extent he will of necessity become a dispensationalist.'[13] Reformed theologians almost universally reject the hermeneutical principle of dispensationalism in eschatology. They reject eschatological conclusions that presuppose literalism – as Ryrie's statement demonstrates, hermeneutical presuppositions drive conclusions.

What is perplexing, however, is that many within the Reformed community will reject dispensational eschatology but embrace its interpretation of creation, or as it is more broadly understood, protology. For example, Presbyterian and Reformed publishes Morris's book on the flood, one of its most popular books; it is in its forty-second printing.[14]

One sees evidence of Morris's dispensationalism throughout his commentary on Genesis. Morris holds to a trichotomous view of man, mediate imputation of original sin, and a restored water canopy during the earthly millennial rule of Christ. He argues that the tree of life had life-prolonging properties and the tree of the knowledge of good and evil toxic genetic-altering

---

[12]Raymond A. Eve and Francis B. Harrold, *The Creationist Movement in Modern America* (Boston: Twayne Publishers, 1991), pp. 46, 51-52; also Ronald L. Numbers, *The Creationists: The Evolution of Scientific Creationism* (Berkeley: University of California Press, 1993), pp. 72-101, 184-213.

[13]Charles Ryrie, *Dispensationalism Today* (1965; Chicago: Moody Press, 1970), p. 51.

[14]John C. Whitcomb and Henry M. Morris, *The Genesis Flood* (1961; Phillipsburg: P & R, 1998).

properties, and he defines *mystery* in a literalistic rather than biblical fashion.[15]

These positions are typical of dispensational theologians, as they are driven by a literalistic hermeneutic. But why do Reformed theologians accept Morris's interpretation of Genesis 1–3 without questioning his presuppositions? Moreover, many in the Reformed community do not even know his hermeneutical presupposition.

In the introduction to his commentary Morris sets forth his interpretive program. He emphasizes not the intended meaning of the text, but a questionable secondary significance. Morris writes:

> The emphasis will be placed primarily on the exposition of the actual events and their historical significance in terms of God's purposes for the world in general, and as principles by which He deals with individuals of all times and places. Typological illustrations will be included where appropriate, but will not constitute the primary emphasis. We wish to stress most of all the real-life truthfulness and significance of this primeval record of man's origin and early history.

It should not pass by unnoticed that Morris gives little thought to typology. What typology does he slight? He ignores Adam as a type of Christ and Eve as a type of the Church.[16] Elsewhere Morris admits the Bible 'is essentially concerned with the first Adam and the second Adam, and the relation between the two'. He nevertheless neglects this central theme of Scripture, indeed of Genesis as well, and treats secondary matters as primary. This methodology leads Morris to write that 'the Bible-believing Christian goes to the Bible for his basic orientation in all departments of truth. The Bible is his textbook of science as well as his guide to spiritual

---

[15]Morris, *Genesis Record*, pp. 61, 75, 87, 88, 102-03, 113.
[16]Morris, *Genesis Record*, pp. 31-32.

truth.' In fact, Morris even says that the tree of the knowledge of good and evil (Gen. 2:9) can be paraphrased as the 'Tree of Science'.[17] Morris labels anyone 'neo-orthodox' who claims that the Bible is theological, not scientific.[18] If one applies a consistently Reformed hermeneutic to the interpretation of Scripture, he must reject Morris's conclusions. Reformed theology neither embraces the Bible as a textbook of science nor employs an overly literalistic hermeneutic. What is it about the other scientific approach that is problematic?

Old Princeton

In Hodge's approach to Genesis, there is a clear path of influence – the geology of the day drove Hodge's exegetical conclusions. This is not a unique observation. Abraham Kuyper criticized Hodge on this very point.[19] What is problematic about Hodge's and Ross' approach is that scientific theory changes. What is in vogue in today's scientific community might soon be on its way out. For example, in 1951 the Roman Catholic Church commended the Big Bang theory and declared that it was in accordance with the Bible. Yet, some scientists now reject the Big Bang theory.[20] As Thomas Kuhn argued, scientific paradigms constantly shift, radically reshaping perceptions of the world.[21] Kuhn observed that Nicholas Copernicus (1473–1543) can be accepted only if Ptolemy (87–150) is wrong, and Albert Einstein (1879–1955) can be accepted only if Isaac Newton (1642–1727) erred.[22]

---

[17]Henry M. Morris, 'The Bible is a Textbook of Science,' *BibSac* 121/4 (1964), p. 345.

[18]Morris, 'Textbook of Science,' p. 341.

[19]Abraham Kuyper, *Principles of Sacred Theology*, trans. J. Hendrik De Vries (1898; Grand Rapids: Baker, 1980), pp. 318-19.

[20]E.g. Steven Hawking, *A Brief History of Time* (1988; New York: Bantam Books, 1996), pp. 49-53.

[21]Thomas S. Kuhn, *The Structure of Scientific Revolutions* (1962; Chicago: University of Chicago Press, 1998), p. ix.

[22]Kuhn, *Scientific Revolutions*, pp. 68, 98; also Alister McGrath, *A Scientific Theology*, vol. 1, *Nature* (Grand Rapids: Eerdmans, 2001), pp. 49, 51.

Moreover, using nature to interpret Scripture inverts the hermeneutical rule that Scripture is its own interpreter, as well as the idea that special revelation interprets general revelation, not vice versa. As the Westminster divines concluded some 350 years ago: 'The infallible rule of interpretation of Scripture is the Scripture itself: and therefore, when there is a question about the true and full sense of any Scripture (which is not manifold, but one), it must be searched and known by other places that speak more clearly' (WCF 1.9). One must therefore reject not only the creation science approach to Genesis, but also the Old Princeton approach.[23] Are there more self-consciously biblical approaches to Genesis 1–3?

Current literalistic approaches to Genesis 1–3
Many in the Reformed community adopt a literal interpretation of Genesis 1–3, which centers its attention upon the length of the days of creation. Literalists claim a long-standing tradition and cite interpreters such as C. F. Keil, H. C. Leupold, Martin Luther, John Calvin, Francis Turretin, Geerhardus Vos, and others.[24] Literalists such as Ligon Duncan and David Hall argue that the literal, or classical, interpretation of Genesis 1–3 dominated from 2000 BC to AD 1800 and that non-literal interpretations of Genesis have arisen

---

[23]This question might arise: If Genesis 1–3 is not about science, how should Christian theology and science interact? The answer lies in a positive development of natural theology. Special revelation, especially Genesis 1–3, should not be twisted into making scientific statements. Rather, special revelation should properly define the limits of natural theology, and from the principles of natural theology develop a positive relationship with the natural sciences (McGrath, *Scientific Theology*, pp. 21, 296). On the historical acceptance of natural theology within the Reformed community see J. V. Fesko and Guy M. Richard, 'Natural Theology and the Westminster Confession,' in *The Westminster Confession into the 21st Century: Essays in Remembrance of the 350th Anniversary of the Westminster Assembly*, vol. 3, ed. J. Ligon Duncan (Fearn: Christian Focus, forthcoming).

[24]Gentry and Butler, *Hath God Said?*, pp. 8-9.

only since the arrival of evolutionary theory.[25] There is a defect, however, with much of the literalist literature on Genesis 1–3. Literalists seem to pay little or no attention to other significant interpretive questions, when this need not be the case. One can affirm the 24-hour view regarding the length of days and yet be exegetically and theologically mindful of more significant events in the text. Some recent explanations of Genesis 1–3 are wanting simply because they focus too much of their exegetical energy on the one issue of the length of days.[26] When exegesis becomes so imbalanced, a re-examination of the most basic questions of interpretation is necessary. One may begin to move through the stalemate in the current literature by asking the question, What is the purpose of Genesis 1–3?

The purpose of Genesis 1–3

Scientific data and world history?
Much of the current literature on Genesis 1–3 claims that the purpose of the three chapters is telling not only that God created but how he created.[27] Morris, for example, writes,

> The Christian polemicist frequently is confronted with the problem of the scientific 'errors' in Scripture, especially in its first eleven chapters. Often he is tempted to resort to the solution of Neo-orthodoxy and to protest that 'the Bible is, after all, not a textbook of science, but rather

---

[25]J. Ligon Duncan and David W. Hall, 'The 24-Hours View,' in *The Genesis Debate*, ed. David G. Hagopian (Mission Viejo: Crux Press, 2001), p. 24; see also Jordan, *Creation*, pp. 10, 17.

[26]There are several volumes dedicated to this one subject: Gentry and Butler, *Hath God Said?*; Jordan, *Creation*; Pipa and Hall, *Did God Create in Six Days?*.

[27]Sid Dyer, 'The New Testament Doctrine of Creation,' in Pipa and Hall, *Did God Create in Six Days?*, p. 237; similarly Young, *Genesis One*, p. 86.

of religion.' 'It is meant to tell us the *fact* of creation, not the *method* of creation; it tells us *who is* Creator, not an understanding of earth history.'[28]

From a different perspective, Ross argues that Genesis 1–11 'is largely scientific' and 'structured like a modern research report'.[29] For Ross, then, Genesis reports about the scientific 'how' of creation. These scientific descriptions of Genesis rest on several presuppositions: (1) Genesis tells the method by which God created the heavens and earth; (2) Genesis 1–11 is about the general history of the earth; and (3) to propose that Genesis 1–11 is about religion, or a theological statement, is the response of neo-orthodoxy, or liberalism. These three points require critique to see the intended purpose of Genesis 1–3.

First, many Christians assume that Genesis 1–2 tells how God created. Yet, when one compares the Genesis account with God's interrogation of Job (Job 38–41), the two passages differ greatly.[30] God asks Job a series of how questions: 'Where were you when I laid the foundation of the earth? Tell me, if you have understanding. Who determined its measurements – surely you know! Or who stretched the line upon it? On what were its bases sunk, or who laid its cornerstone?' (Job 38:4-6). Of the sixty-plus questions about the creation that God asks Job, none receives an answer. On this point, Derek Thomas writes that 'Job, of course, was not around when God made the world. He knew nothing of how the earth was made (38:4-7), or how the sea was formed (38:8-11), or how the planetary rotations constitute day and night (38:12-15, 19-21).'[31] God asks the volley of questions

---

[28]Morris, 'Textbook of Science,' p. 341.

[29]Hugh Ross, *The Genesis Question* (1998; Colorado Springs: NavPress, 2001), pp. 8, 19.

[30]Hermann Gunkel, *Genesis*, trans. Mark E. Biddle (Macon: Mercer UP, 1997), p. 118.

[31]Derek Thomas, *The Storm Breaks: Job Simply Explained* (Durham: Evangelical Press, 1995), p. 291.

regarding the how of creation to prove that Job does not know how the Lord created the world. If one assumes the common interpretive theory on Genesis 1–2, Job could have replied to God, 'Yes! I do know. I've read Genesis!' Job, of course, assuming he lived during the time of Moses, would not have done this even if Genesis 1–2 did provide the how of creation.

This point becomes clearer when one examines rabbinic interpretation of the creation account:

> For it is written, 'In the beginning God created the heaven.' But it is not explained how. Where then is it explained? Elsewhere: That stretches out the heavens as a curtain (Isa. 40:22); 'and the earth,' which is likewise not explained. Where is that explained? Elsewhere: For He says to the snow: Fall on the earth, etc. (Job 37:6). 'And God said: Let there be light' (1:3), and the manner of this, too, is not explained. Where is it explained? Elsewhere: Who covers himself with light as with a garment (Psa. 104:2). (*Mid. Rabb.* Gen. 1.6)

While there is question concerning the interpretation of these passages (e.g. Isa. 40:22; Job 37:6; Ps. 104:2), the author does not see in Genesis 1 how God created but instead looks elsewhere in Scripture to answer this question.

The answers to many of God's questions to Job, at least scientifically, lie not in Scripture but in the scientific investigation of nature. Thomas explains that, 'Today, great advances have been made in understanding some of these questions: the earth's rotation (38:12-15), oceanic currents (38:16), cartography (38:18), the origin and dispersal of light (38:19, 24) and meteorology (38:28-30, 35). These questions anticipate the great scientific advances made by such men as Newton, Maury, Faraday and Morse.'[32] The common idea that Genesis speaks to the 'how' of creation, therefore, is

---

[32]Thomas, *Storm Breaks*, p. 291.

misguided. Yes, Genesis is historical – but its intended purpose is not to convey scientific information.[33] The Westminster divines long ago observed that Scripture is not scientific but that 'the scriptures principally teach, what man is to believe concerning God, and what duty God requires of man' (Larger Catechism 5). Building upon this historically Reformed approach to the Scriptures Paul Woolley writes that a

> serious misapprehension concerning the Scripture is that the Holy Spirit so inspired the writers as to cause them to use modern scientific canons in their use of language. For example, it is argued that, when the inspired writer said, 'it is he that sits above the circle of the earth' (Isa. 40:22), there is in this form of statement a reference to the sphericity of the earth. Such an interpretation is mistaken for several reasons. a) Revelation came to an inspired writer for a specific purpose. Scripture was not written by mechanical dictation and God did not reveal to its writers truths quite irrelevant to the purpose in hand. The prophet at this particular point had no need of a revelation concerning the shape of the earth. b) The writer often, as we shall see, did not understand the entire import of his writing but he was not writing what were to himself obscure conundrums, and the interpreter of Scripture must not read into it meanings of an entirely different genus from those of the writer. The author here doubtless had in mind the rough circle visible to an observer from a point elevated above the earth's surface. He was not talking about astronomical truth at all. c) Figurative forms of expression, when they appear in the Bible, are to be recognized as such and not interpreted as natural science. [34]

---

[33]Nahum M. Sarna, *Understanding Genesis* (New York: McGraw-Hill, 1966), p. 3; Bruce K. Waltke, *Genesis: A Commentary* (Grand Rapids: Zondervan, 2001), pp. 73-77, 80; Walter Brueggemann, *Theology of the Old Testament* (Minneapolis: Fortress, 1997), p. 528.

[34]Paul Woolley, 'The Relevancy of Scripture,' in *The Infallible Word*, eds. N. B. Stonehouse and Paul Woolley (1946; Phillipsburg: P & R, 2002), pp. 203-04.

Woolley basically sets forth the historical Reformed approach to the interpretation of Scripture, which is the use of the *analogia fidei* or *Scripturae*, the analogy of faith or Scripture, not the canons of science. In this connection Henri Blocher writes: 'In the case of the opening chapters of Genesis, it is not plausible that the human author knew what we are taught by astronomers, geologists and other scientists. Therefore we must curb the desire to make the scientific view play a part in the actual interpretation; the interpretation must cling solely to the text and its context.'[35]

Second, contrary to Morris's claim, Genesis 1–11 is not about world history. Morris seems to imply that God set up a camcorder and taped everything that took place. Yet this type of interpretation ignores the details, particularly what is absent from the opening chapters of Genesis. For example, Genesis 1 includes nothing regarding the creation of angels or the fall of Satan. Furthermore, Genesis 4 leaves the reader with the impression that there are only four people on the earth: Adam, Eve, Cain, and Abel. Cain, however, kills Abel, leaves, marries, and builds a city. From where does Cain's wife originate? Cities require people; it is hardly a city if the only inhabitants are Cain and his wife. Contrary to the claim of Morris, Genesis 1–11 is a selective history – it does not deal with general world history but redemptive history, the *historia salutis*.[36]

Third, contrary to the claim of Morris, to say that Genesis 1–11 is primarily a religious or theological work is not akin to neo-orthodoxy. This claim fails for two reasons: (a) Morris does not demonstrate any error from the writings of neo-orthodox theologians who claim that

---

[35]Henri Blocher, *In the Beginning: The Opening Chapters of Genesis*, trans. David G. Preston (Downers Grove: InterVarsity Press, 1984), pp. 26-27.
[36]Woolley, 'Relevancy of Scripture,' p. 207.

the Bible is primarily theological; this is problematic. Even if neo-orthodox theologians claim that Genesis 1–11 is primarily theological, it does not automatically mean that the claim is incorrect. This is the genetic fallacy, assuming error because of a questionable source. (b) Theologians outside of the neo-orthodox camp have made the same claim. It was R. L. Dabney who wrote:

> When revelation says anything concerning material nature, it is only what is made necessary to the comprehension of theological fact or doctrine. And in its observance of this distinction the Bible is eminently a practical book, saying nothing whatever for mere curiosity, and stopping at just what is essential to religious truth. Hence, we ought to understand that when the Scriptures use popular language to describe physical occurrences or facts, all they mean is to state the apparent phenomena as they would seem to the popular eye to occur. They never intended to give us the non-apparent scientific mechanism of those facts or occurrences; for this is not essential to their practical object, and is left to the philosopher. Hence, when natural science comes and teaches us that the true *rationale* of apparent phenomena is different from that which seems to be suggested by the terms of Scripture and of popular language, there is no real contradiction between science and the Bible or between science and the popular phraseology.

Dabney criticizes both Roman Catholic and Protestant scientific misuse of Scripture. He states that for 'the doctors of Salamanca to condemn Columbus' geography as unscriptural and the inquisition and Turretin to argue against the astronomy of Galileo, as infidel, was mistaken'. Roman Catholic theologians argued that the Psalms speak of the heavens spread out like a canopy and the earth as unmovable and extended (Ps. 104:2; 93:1), and that the Copernican theory of heliocentricity was false because the Scriptures speak of the earth as established and the sun moving in its circuit across the heavens (Ps. 19:6). Dabney condemns this as 'exegetical folly'.[37] Dabney was not alone in limiting the purpose of Scripture to speak to theological issues. For example, Calvin, commenting on Psalm 136:7, 'To him who made great lights,' writes: 'The Holy Spirit had no intention to teach astronomy.'[38] Genesis 1–11, more specifically 1–3, is therefore not about science and does not direct the reader to scientific data.[39] Rather, Genesis 1–3 is theological. What theological message, then, does Genesis 1–3 communicate?

Christological focus and purpose

The emphasis of Scripture is not generically theological but christological. Though taking note of the problematic christomonism that often colors neo-orthodoxy, it is appropriate to observe that Emil Brunner nevertheless correctly argues that

> the uniqueness of this Christian doctrine of Creation and the Creator is continually being obscured by the fact that theologians are so reluctant to begin their work with the New Testament; when they want to deal with the Creation, they tend to begin with the Old Testament, although they never do this when they are speaking of the Redeemer. The emphasis on the story of Creation at the beginning of the Bible has constantly led theologians to forsake the rule which they would otherwise follow, namely, that the basis of *all* Christian articles of faith is the Incarnate Word, Jesus Christ. So when we begin to study the subject of Creation in the Bible we ought to start with the first chapter of the Gospel of John, and

---

[37] Robert L. Dabney, *The Life and Letters of Robert Lewis Dabney*, ed. Thomas Cary Johnson (Edinburgh: Banner of Truth, 1977), p. 342.

[38] John Calvin, *Commentary on the Psalms*, CTS, trans. James Anderson (1849; Grand Rapids: Baker, 1993), p. 184.

[39] Young, *Genesis One*, pp. 43, 54.

some other passages of the *New* Testament, and not with the first chapter of Genesis.[40]

This is an important interpretive presupposition, namely, the christological connection to the opening chapters of Genesis. Primarily, Genesis 1–3 is not about science, or the history of the world, but is the entry point to the person and work of Christ. On this point Alister McGrath similarly notes that

> before setting out the concepts of creation found in the Old Testament, it is important to establish a fundamental point of interpretation. For Christians, the Old Testament is to be read in the light of the New Testament, and especially in the light of Christ. Scripture centers on and enfolds Christ, who can be known definitively only through its medium.[41]

Christology informs Genesis 1–3 and therefore one must constantly interpret these chapters in the light of the New Testament.

E. J. Young explains the importance of the connection between Genesis 1 and christology, writing that the Bible

> always places the creation in the light of the central fact of redemption, Christ Jesus. When we examine the first chapter of Genesis in the light of other parts of Scripture, it becomes clear that the intention is not to give a survey of the process of creation, but to permit us to see the creative activity of God in the light of his saving acts, and so, in its structure, the chapter allows its full light to fall upon man, the crown of the creative work.[42]

---

[40]Emil Brunner, *The Christian Doctrine of Creation and Redemption* (London: Lutterwork Press, 1952), p. 6; cf. Richard A. Muller, 'Emmanuel V. Gerhart on the "Christ-Idea" as Fundamental Principle,' *WTJ* 48/1 (1986), pp. 97-117.

[41]McGrath, *Scientific Theology*, p. 142.

[42]Young, *Genesis*, p. 45.

Why is it, for example, that the New Testament is replete with phrases and imagery taken from the opening chapters of Genesis, such as light and darkness (John 1:1ff), Christ as creator (Col. 1:16), or Christ as the second Adam (Rom. 5:12-19, 1 Cor. 15:45)? The answer lies in the purpose of Genesis 1-3. Genesis 1-3 should not be interpreted in isolation, but in the light of the New Testament, in the light of Christ. Genesis 1-3 sets forth the theological significance of the failed work of the first Adam, which serves as the entry point for the successful work of the second Adam, Jesus Christ. Genesis 1-3 must be approached in the light of Christ. In order to understand rightly the christological message of Genesis 1-3, what should mark one's interpretive methodology?

Interpretive methodology: christology and eschatology
Many come at Genesis 1-3 in terms of the length of the days, science, old-earth or young-earth. Others treat it as merely an account of the origins of the physical world: Genesis simply reports the creation of the stage, the physical world, upon which the drama of redemption unfolds.[43] Genesis 1-3, however, does not record merely the construction of the stage but rather shows in shadows and types the person and work of Christ. This christological approach to the interpretation of the Old Testament is not new but has excellent scriptural precedence. When Christ was on the road to Emmaus with his two disciples 'beginning with Moses and all the Prophets, he interpreted to them in all the Scriptures the things concerning himself' (Luke 24:27). Likewise, Paul calls Adam 'a type of the one who was to come' (Rom. 5:14). This interpretive trajectory of the New Testament is why the Reformed community has placed such a premium upon the typological interpretation of

---

[43]So Francis Watson, *Text and Truth: Redefining Biblical Theology* (Grand Rapids: Eerdmans, 1997), pp. 232, 237-39.

the Old Testament. In this regard the Westminster divines explain the relationship between the Old Testament and New Testament as it pertains to the covenant of grace:

> This covenant was differently administered in the time of the law, and in the time of the gospel; under the law it was administered by promises, prophecies, sacrifices, circumcision, the paschal lamb, and other types and ordinances delivered to the people of the Jews, all foresignifying Christ to come, which were for that time sufficient and efficacious, through the operation of the Spirit, to instruct and build up the elect in faith in the promised Messiah, by whom they had full remission of sins, and eternal salvation; and is called the Old Testament (WCF 7.5).

One must note that according to the divines the Old Testament foresignifies Christ to come. This is why Genesis 1–3 must be interpreted by searching for the connections between the work of the first and second Adams. Moreover, the investigation should be broadened by treating Genesis 1–3, not under the systematic theological subject of creation, but under the broader category of protology. In fact, this essay represents a desire to alter permanently the traditional loci of systematic theology and add the locus of protology. Why?

Most systematic theological treatments of Genesis 1–3 include these chapters in the doctrine of creation, which entails the creation of the physical world *ex nihilo*, anthropology, constitution of man, *imago Dei*, fall, and perhaps the covenant of works.[44] When one examines

---

[44]E.g. Hodge, *Systematic Theology*, vol. 1, pp. 550-74; Robert L. Reymond, *A New Systematic Theology of the Christian Faith* (Nashville: Thomas Nelson, 1998), pp. 383ff; Millard J. Erickson, *Christian Theology* (Grand Rapids: Baker, 1985), pp. 365-86; Louis Berkhof, *Systematic Theology* (1938; Grand Rapids: Baker, 1996), pp. 126-80; Wayne Grudem, *Systematic Theology* (Grand Rapids: Zondervan, 1994), pp. 439-528.

Genesis 1–3 from the systematic theological perspective, he sees a picture almost exclusively through the lens of ontology. It is perhaps this ontological lens that has led to the fragmented reading of Genesis 1–3, namely, examining the opening chapters of Scripture almost strictly in terms of the origin of man vis-à-vis Darwinian evolution. This fragmentary reading, in turn, has led to the misuse of Genesis in the battle between the claims of Darwin and the teachings of the Bible.

While it is true that Genesis teaches the origins of man, this fact cannot be separated from redemptive history. One can only understand anthropology in light of the true man, Jesus Christ. The work of the second Adam teaches the significance of the first Adam, and vice versa. For example, the *munus triplex,* Christ as prophet, priest, and king, does not emerge in the middle of the Old Testament but in the initial chapters of Genesis. Adam is the first prophet, priest, and king. He was the first prophet, in that he was given the command of God to propagate, not to eat of the tree of knowledge. He was the first priest, in that he was to tend and keep the garden, the first temple, God's dwelling place among his people. And, he was the first king, in that he was given the dominion mandate to rule as God's vicegerent.

Redemptive history as a whole, then, necessitates exploring Genesis 1–3 in terms of protology rather than creation. Moreover, one must recognize the connections between protology and eschatology, connections that have important implications for the interpretation of Genesis 1–3.

The completed work of the second Adam appears in the final chapters of Revelation, or in the eschatological context. If the second Adam takes up the work of the first Adam, then eschatology has an irrefragable connection to the beginning, or protology. This connection becomes even clearer when one considers that the categories of the beginning are embedded in eschatology, the creation of the heavens and earth become the *new* heavens and earth

(Isa. 65:17; 66:22) and the garden of Eden reappears in the book of Revelation (2:7; cf. Isa. 51:3; Zech. 1:17).[45] The broader category of protology enables one to consider matters of ontology, or systematic theology, but also redemptive history, or biblical theology.[46] Under this broader rubric of protology one can see the connections between anthropology and christology, the first and second Adams, and protology and eschatology, Genesis and Revelation, the beginning and the end, the alpha and omega.[47] When one interprets Genesis 1–3, however, he cannot bypass the important spade work of interpreting the significance of the narrative within its original historical context.

Immediate historical context

Governing interpretation are two horizons: the immediate historical context of the fifteenth century BC and the greater amount of information given by progressive revelation. In other words, one must enter the world of the original audience but also examine Genesis 1–3 in the light of the revelation of Jesus Christ.[48] Because Moses is the essential author of Genesis, one can therefore place the composition of Genesis sometime during the Israelite exodus from Egypt or wilderness wandering.[49]

---

[45]Walter C. Kaiser and Moisés Silva, *An Introduction to Biblical Hermeneutics* (Grand Rapids: Zondervan, 1994), p. 151.

[46]Neither systematic nor biblical theology should eclipse each other in the interpretive process (see Carl R. Trueman, 'A Revolutionary Balancing Act,' *Themelios* 27/3 [2002], pp. 1-4; also similarly Geerhardus Vos, 'The Idea of Biblical Theology as a Science and as a Theological Discipline,' in *Redemptive History and Biblical Interpretation*, ed. Richard B. Gaffin, Jr. [Phillipsburg: P & R, 1980], pp. 3-24, esp. pp. 23-24).

[47]Wolfhart Pannenberg, *Systematic Theology*, vol. 2, trans. Geoffrey W. Bromiley (Grand Rapids: Eerdmans, 1991), p. 146; similarly Geerhardus Vos, *Biblical Theology* (1948; Edinburgh: Banner of Truth, 1996), p. 28; McGrath, *Scientific Theology*, pp. 186, 191.

[48]Thomas R. Schreiner, *Paul: Apostle of God's Glory in Christ* (Downers Grover: InterVarsity Press, 2001), p. 31.

[49]Contra, e.g. Brueggemann, *Theology of the OT*, p. 533. On the

This situation provides context as well as information about the intended audience. The Israelites had left Egypt, a land given over to idolatry and paganism; they were preparing to enter the promised land, a land occupied by idolaters and pagans. If this is the setting, far from calculating the age of the universe, the Genesis account reminded the Israelites of the character and attributes of the God they serve.

For example, Egyptian priests promoted the worship of the sun, moon, birds, sea creatures, cats, elephants, and bulls.[50] Because God created all of these, Genesis 1–2 reminded the Israelites coming out of Egypt that these so-called gods were creatures. Likewise, the creation account reminded the Israelites, as they entered a land occupied by Baal worshipers, that all blessings came from God. Fred Woods notes that

> when the Hebrew tribes left the stable environment of Egypt and headed toward the land of Canaan, they encountered a people who worshipped the storm god called Baal and his retinue. Such an encounter created a culture conflict. Israel had been led by Yahweh through the sea and the desert, but as she entered the new land, Israel asked, 'Was Yahweh also the god of Canaan?' As the Israelites settled in Canaan, they were tempted to ask their Canaanite neighbors, 'How does your garden grow?' Such inquiry was seen by later writers as having led to eventual apostasy and exile as Israel became idolatrous and eventually drowned in Baalism.[51]

Mosaic essential authorship of the Pentateuch see Gleason Archer, *A Survey of Old Testament Introduction* (1964; Chicago: Moody Press, 1985), pp. 109-24; Raymond B. Dillard and Tremper Longman III, *An Introduction to the Old Testament* (Grand Rapids: Zondervan, 1994), pp. 38-40; cf. Peter Enns, 'William Henry Green and the Authorship of the Pentateuch: Some Historical Considerations,' *JETS* 45/3 (2002), pp. 385-403.

[50]John D. Currid, *Ancient Egypt and the Old Testament* (Grand Rapids: Baker, 1997), pp. 109-17.

[51]Fred E. Woods, *Water and Storm Polemics Against Baalism in the Deuteronomic History* (New York: Peter Lang, 1994), p. 2; similarly

Against this backdrop, the creation account displays a theological purpose. For example, God sends rain, not Baal: 'When no bush of the field was yet in the land and no small plant of the field had yet sprung up – for the LORD God had not caused it to rain on the land' (Gen. 2:5). Throughout the Old Testament this struggle recurs and culminates with the showdown between Elijah and the prophets of Baal. God created a drought (1 Kings 17:1) and then caused it to rain (1 Kings 18:45). In fact, the Pentateuch confirms these points (Deut. 4:15-19). In Deuteronomy 4.15-19 Moses warns against worshiping the creation. Likewise, in Deuteronomy 11:10-17 Moses reminds Israel who is the source of agricultural success, Yahweh.

All of this textual evidence suggests that one should analyze the creation account not with a view to twenty-first-century scientific questions but rather in the theological and religious context of the Israelite exodus and conquest of the promised land.[52] But one must look further. The proximate significance of Genesis 1–3 is theological and bound to its immediate historical context, its ultimate significance is christological. The text's meaning does not change from one context to the next, but as revelation progresses the ultimate significance becomes clearer. For example, the reader has hints of God's triunity in Genesis 1:26, but this only becomes clear in the New Testament. Moreover, the text states that God created in Genesis 1 but the New Testament teaches that Christ created (Col. 1:16ff). One must therefore keep the immediate historical context in sight as well as its ultimate and christological significance. As the Westminster divines stated, the Old

---

Nahum Sarna, *Genesis*, JPSTC (Philadelphia: JPS, 1989), pp. 3-4. For a comparison between the cosmogonies of the ANE and Genesis see Victor P. Hamilton, *Handbook on the Pentateuch* (Grand Rapids: Baker, 1993), pp. 33ff.

[52]See Meredith G. Kline, *Structure of Biblical Authority* (Eugene: Wipf & Stock, 1989), pp. 53-57.

Testament foresignifies Christ. There is one last issue to consider.

Sources and method of investigation

In the course of the investigation a vast array of sources will be utilized, including the Scriptures themselves using the *analogia fidei*, extant documents contemporaneous with both the Old Testament and New Testament, rabbinic interpretation, ancient Christian sources from the patristic, medieval, Reformation, post-Reformation, and contemporary periods. Moreover, the insights of commentators from a variety of perspectives, liberal and conservative, will be used. Using this vast array of sources is important for several reasons.

First, one must use the Scriptures themselves, as *sacra Scriptura est sui interpres*, or holy Scripture is its own interpreter. As previously stated, many fail to use the analogy of Scripture when it comes to Genesis 1–3. What does the rest of Scripture have to say about the opening chapters of the Bible?

Second, documents from the same historical context, such as the *Enuma Elish* or Hittite covenants, give a background for Genesis 1–3.[53]

Third, ancient Jewish sources from the Qumran community and rabbinic interpretation at points illuminate what the original audience might have understood. Just as commentaries offer good insights, so also commentaries from ancient sources help the reader understand the text.

Fourth, an array of commentaries ancient and contemporary, liberal and conservative, prove useful for two reasons: (1) the Holy Spirit has never restricted himself to one geographic place or one manifestation of the Church; and (2) even on the general level, the Bible, in its perspicuity, is a book made up of nouns, verbs, adverbs, sentences, paragraphs and so on. One must

---

[53]Hamilton, *Pentateuch*, p. 35.

allow that even an unbeliever can read the Bible and comprehend its message at an intellectual level, and therefore offer some insight.[54] Yet an unbeliever cannot create belief or regenerate himself through the power of intellect. Only the Holy Spirit can create belief in the heart and mind of an unbeliever.

Conclusion

One may now proceed to investigate Genesis 1–3. The reader should keep in mind that the hermeneutical presuppositions of this investigation include: the analogy of Scripture, analyzing the contextual historical information, and examining Genesis 1–3 in the light of the second Adam, or christology, and eschatology. The overall thesis of this essay is that Genesis 1–3 is not about science or world history but about the failed work of the first Adam, a fact which points the reader to the person and work of the second, or eschatological, Adam. The patterns in Genesis 1–3 recur throughout redemptive history and reappear in the eschaton with the revelation of Christ on the final day. Genesis 1–3 must be read, therefore, eschatologically and christologically in order to understand its ultimate significance. The investigation will proceed by first examining the creation of man in the image of God. From there the study will examine the nature of the garden of Eden, the work of the first Adam, namely the covenant of works, shadows and types of the second Adam, the second Adam and his work, and finally conclude with the Sabbath.

---

[54]See Kaiser and Silva, *Biblical Hermeneutics*, pp. 20-25.

1

MAN IN THE IMAGE OF GOD

Introduction

The first part of the investigation of Genesis 1–3 begins with an exploration of the creation of man in the image of God. Many approach this issue solely in terms of creation, fall, and restoration. In other words, most approach the image of God in terms of the *ordo salutis*.[1] While one must certainly explore this subject in terms of the *ordo salutis*, what many do not realize are the redemptive historical considerations bound up in the image of God. If the first Adam is created in the image of God and the second Adam, Jesus Christ, is the image of God, then the overall message of Scripture is that though man was made in the image of God and lost it through the fall, the image of God will be restored to fallen man through the work of the second Adam. This is no more evident than when Paul writes: 'Just as we have borne the image of the man of dust, we shall also bear the image of the man

---

[1]So Francis Turretin, *Institutes of Elenctic Theology*, 3 vols., ed. James T. Dennison, trans. George Musgrave Giger (Phillipsburg: P & R, 1992-97), 5.10, pp. 464-70; Charles Hodge, *Systematic Theology* (1889; Grand Rapids: Eerdmans, 1993), pp. 96-103; R. L. Dabney, *Systematic Theology* (1878; Edinburgh: Banner of Truth, 1996), pp. 293-98; Robert L. Reymond, *A New Systematic Theology of the Christian Faith* (Nashville: Thomas Nelson, 1998), pp. 425-30; Wayne Grudem, *Systematic Theology* (Grand Rapids: Zondervan, 1994), pp. 442-50; Louis Berkhof, *Systematic Theology: New Combined Edition* (1932-41; Grand Rapids: Eerdmans, 1996), pp. 202-10.

of heaven' (1 Cor. 15:49). Paul's statement means that in order to have a comprehension of what it means for man to be created in the image of God, one cannot stop with the Genesis creation narratives but must begin with the presupposition of the eschatological Adam, Jesus Christ, as the image of God. This chapter will therefore explore the Genesis narrative as it pertains to man's creation in the image of God and then explore its significance in terms of the second Adam.

When one enters upon the subject of the image of God the typical starting point is Genesis 1:26: 'Then God said, "Let us make man in our image, after our likeness. And let them have dominion over the fish of the sea and over the birds of the heavens and over the livestock and over all the earth and over every creeping thing that creeps on the earth."' Scholars have spilled much ink over the use of plural pronouns in this verse: 'let us make man in our image.' There are of course two major questions packed into this little phrase: (1) why does God speak in the plural and (2) what does it mean to be made in the image of God?[2] Understanding the nature of God will assist in the definition of God's image. In other words, Is God triune, and does the image of God in man reflect God's triunity?

The nature of God
At least three explanations have been offered for the text's use of the plural: (1) God speaks to his heavenly court; (2) it is a plural of majesty; or (3) it is an inchoate reference to the Trinity.[3]

---

[2]Gordon J. Wenham, *Genesis 1-15*, WBC, vol. 1 (Dallas: Word, 1987), p. 27.

[3]Kidner argues that this phrase is a plural of fullness because it is linked with the plural noun אלהים ('ĕlōhîm) (Derek Kidner, *Genesis*, TOTC [Downers Grove: Intervarsity, 1967], pp. 51-52). Similarly, Westermann argues that it is the plural of deliberation, which is 'a form of speech which occurred primarily in self-deliberation' (Claus Westermann, *Genesis 1-11*, trans. John J. Scullion [Minneapolis: Fortress, 1994], p. 145).

Option 1: Heavenly court. From the earliest times rabbinic interpreters thought that God was addressing his heavenly court.[4] There are glimpses of the heavenly court in various parts of Scripture: the seraphim, cherubim, and elders that surround the throne of God (Isa. 6:2-6; Rev. 4:4).[5] A recent advocate of this position is Meredith Kline.[6] Kline argues that God addresses his heavenly court based upon several passages of Scripture (Gen. 3:22-24; 18:21–19.1; Isa. 6:2-8). Kline explains that these verses demonstrate that when God speaks in the plural, it is in the presence of his heavenly court, and even when he speaks in the singular, he often sends multiple representatives, as in the case of the judgment against Sodom.[7] Others have argued that God speaks in a plural of majesty.[8]

Option 2: Plural of majesty. C. F. Keil argues that verse 26 is 'God speaking of Himself and with Himself in the plural of number' and 'with reference to the fullness of the divine powers and essences which He possesses'.[9]

---

[4]Gerhard von Rad, *Genesis*, OTL (Philadelphia: Westminster, 1972), p. 58; Nahum Sarna, *Genesis*, JPSTC (Philadelphia: JPS, 1989), p. 12; Umberto Cassuto, *Genesis*, Part One, *Adam to Noah*, trans. Israel Abrahams (Jerusalem: Magnes, 1998), p. 55; see *Mid. Rabb.* Gen. 8.3; 17.4.

[5]Wenham, *Genesis*, p. 27. Though Gunkel holds this view, his understanding is colored by the presupposition of the documentary hypothesis. In other words, the ancient Israelites were originally polytheistic and comfortable with the idea that there were other elohim-beings (Herman Gunkel, *Genesis*, trans. Mark Biddle [Macon: Mercer UP, 1997], p. 112). Driving Gunkel's opinion are the parallels in ANE cosmogonies such as the *Enuma Elish*: '[Marduk] opened his mouth and unto Ea he spake. That which he had conceived in his heart he imparted unto him: "My blood will I take and bone will I fashion. I will make man ..."' (Tablet 6.3-6a).

[6]See also W. Randall Garr, *In His Own Image and Likeness: Humanity, Divinity, and Monotheism* (Leiden: Brill, 2003), pp. 51-92.

[7]Meredith Kline, *Images of the Spirit* (Eugene: Wipf & Stock, 1998), pp. 22-23; so also Sarna, *Genesis*, p. 12.

[8]See Garr, *Image and Likeness*, pp. 23-49.

[9]C. F. Keil and Franz Delitzsch, *Commentary on the Old Testament*, 10 vols. (1866-91; Peabody: Hendrickson, 1996), vol. 1, p. 39.

Though Keil allows for trinitarian implications, he argues that the primary force is in the plural of majesty, something like the royal 'we' in English.[10] Similarly, though uninterested in trinitarian implications, Umberto Cassuto considers verse 26 a plural of exhortation, 'Let us go!'[11]

Option 3: The Trinity. Gordon Wenham notes that this verse has traditionally been cited as a proof-text for the Trinity but says 'it is now universally admitted that this was not what the plural meant to the original author.'[12] Yet this is not necessarily so. Early Jewish explanations of this passage saw the tension between the singular subject and the plural verb, 'Then God said [sg.], "Let us make [pl.] man in our image."' The book of Jubilees, written in the second century BC, gives an account of the creation of man based upon Genesis where the plural verb disappears: 'And after this, he created man, a man and a woman created he them' (Jub. 2.14). The Talmud likewise recognizes this tension and argues that because Genesis 1:27 refers to one God, Genesis 1:26 must also refer to one God. So, Jewish interpreters recognized the grammatical tension and sought to eliminate it. In other words, the author and original audience most likely saw the oddity of the verse.[13] While the author might not have understood the complete implications of the grammatical tension, it could be an adumbration of the essential unity yet plurality of the Godhead.[14] This is certainly a possibility given the progressive revelation of God as triune from the Old Testament to the New. In

---

[10]Wenham, *Genesis*, p. 28.

[11]Cassuto, *Genesis*, p. 55.

[12]Wenham, *Genesis*, p. 27. For a cross-section of views from the church fathers see Andrew Louth, ed., *Genesis 1-11*, ACCS (Downers Grove: InterVarsity, 2001), pp. 27ff.

[13]Garr, *Image and Likeness*, p. 18.

[14]Millard Erickson, *God in Three Persons* (Grand Rapids: Baker, 1995), pp. 167-68.

other words, while one must acknowledge the human author's intention, he must also remember that God is the ultimate author (2 Tim. 3:16). God, for example, often revealed more to his prophets than they themselves understood (1 Pet. 1:10-11). Of the three options, which is the best?

The best option is that Genesis 1:26 is an adumbration of the Trinity. Why is this the best option? The problem with the heavenly court argument is with the words 'in our image, after our likeness.' Man was created in the image of God alone (v. 27), and neither in the image of angels nor God and the angels. This view would also imply that the heavenly court participated in the creation of man. The rest of Scripture does not state that angels or other heavenly intermediaries participated in the creation. Additionally, considering the use of בָּרָא (Bârâ') in verse 27, this verb is used only of direct creative acts by God, not other heavenly beings. God alone, therefore, is the agent of creation.[15]

If Genesis 1:26 is a plural of majesty as Keil suggests, then why did early Jewish interpreters seek to eliminate the grammatical tension in the verse? The concept of a plural of majesty might be more a part of Keil's context than a part of the author's context. Millard Erickson notes that 'if this is to be interpreted as a plural of majesty, we must conclude that God uses the plural of majesty while the author of this passage does not, which would seem most peculiar, if the Jews were familiar with and used the plural of majesty.'[16] Martin Luther brusquely comments: 'It is utterly ridiculous when the Jews say that God is following the custom of princes, who, to indicate respect, speak of themselves in the plural number. The Holy Spirit is not imitating this court mannerism (to give it this name); nor does Holy

---

[15]Keil, *Comm. on the OT*, vol. 1, p. 38; H. C. Leupold, *Genesis*, vol. 1 (Grand Rapids: Baker, 1958), p. 87.
[16]Erickson, *God in Three Persons*, p. 168.

Scripture sanction this manner of speech.'[17] Hermann Gunkel also noted that the plural of majesty was first introduced by the Persians, long after the composition of Genesis (see Ezra 4:18; 1 Macc. 10.19).[18] Options 1 and 2 may therefore be eliminated. This leaves the third option as the strongest contender, an adumbration of or inchoate reference to the Trinity.

It is not impossible that verse 26 is an inchoate reference to the Trinity, contra Wenham. Wenham argues that this interpretation would not be possible because it would be 'beyond the horizon of the editor of Genesis', but this idea does not stand up to close scrutiny.[19] Genesis 1:2 mentions the involvement of the Holy Spirit in creation, and Colossians 1:16-17 states that Jesus Christ also participated in the event of creation, yet Genesis mentions little to nothing about their involvement. The author may not have been aware of Christ's involvement, but later revelation makes it clear. He would, however, know of the Spirit's involvement from Genesis 1:2. A similar pattern emerges in other portions of Genesis: the *protoevangelium* (Gen. 3.15) is a reference to Christ's victory over Satan, yet it is quite possible that the author was unaware of exactly how this would come to pass.

Moreover, the reader should not make too many assumptions regarding what the author may or may not have known. Enoch, for example, prophesied about the second advent of Christ (Jude 14). Regardless, just because the original audience may not have understood the full implications of a passage of Scripture does not mean that it can not have a *sensus plenior*. The New Testament often sheds greater revelatory light and increases understanding of difficult Old Testament passages. Along these lines, Luther writes:

---

[17]Martin Luther, *Lectures on Genesis*, LW, vol.1, ed. Jaroslav Pelikan (St. Louis: Concordia, 1958), p. 58.

[18]Gunkel, *Genesis*, p. 112; also Garr, *Image and Likeness*, p. 20.

[19]Wenham, *Genesis*, p. 28.

Therefore what had previously been taught through enigmas, as it were, Christ made clear and commanded to be preached in plain language. The holy patriarchs had this knowledge through the Holy Spirit, although not with such clarity as now, when we hear mentioned in the New Testament the Father, the Son, and the Holy Spirit.[20]

Hence, in the light of the New Testament, this seems to be the best of the three options: Genesis 1:26 is a reference to the Trinity.[21] Had the New Testament not thrown light upon this passage, readers of Scripture might not have fully grasped Genesis 1:26 as a reference to the Trinity.[22] What the author or original audience actually knew, however, is beyond the reader's grasp. It is possible that the author was aware of the trinitarian imp-ications of verse 26 in some rudimentary form. That the triune God makes man in his own image is signif-icant, as man therefore reflects the unity and plurality of the Godhead. As Anthony Hoekema writes, 'Human beings reflect God, who exists not as a solitary being but as a being in fellowship – a fellowship that is described at a later stage of divine revelation as that between the Father, the Son, and the Holy Spirit.'[23] Moving forward, one must determine what comprises the image of the triune God.

---

[20]Luther, *Genesis*, p. 59.

[21]John Calvin, *Genesis*, CTS, trans. John King (1847; Grand Rapids: Baker, 1993), p. 92; Leupold, *Genesis*, pp. 86ff; Karl Barth, *Church Dogmatics*, vol. 3.1, *The Doctrine of Creation*, trans. J. W. Edwards, et al. (1958; Edinburgh: T & T Clark, 1998), p. 192; Victor P. Hamilton, *Handbook on the Pentateuch* (Grand Rapids: Baker, 1982), p. 23; Robert Letham, *The Holy Trinity: In Scripture, History, Theology, and Worship* (Phillipsburg: P & R, 2005), pp. 20-21.

[22]Leupold, *Genesis*, p. 88.

[23]Anthony A. Hoekema, *Created in God's Image* (Grand Rapids: Eerdmans, 1986), p. 14.

The image and likeness of God

Different definition options
What does it mean to be created in the image and likeness of God? צֶלֶם (selem), image, is found in fifteen places in the Old Testament. It appears in Genesis 5.3 where the text states that Adam 'fathered a son in his own likeness, after his image, and named him Seth.' It is also used of models of hemorrhoids (1 Sam. 6:5 MT), pictures of men (Ezek. 16:17), or idols (Num. 33:52). דְּמוּת (Dmût), likeness, is used for a model or plan (1 Kings 16:10). It is also frequently used in Ezekiel and translated as 'something like.'[24] What do these words say about the image and likeness of God as it is found in man, male and female? As with many challenging verses, there are several interpretive options:

1. Image and likeness are distinct. Image refers to the natural qualities in man (e.g. reason, personality) while likeness refers to the supernatural graces that make redeemed man godlike. This was the view of the early church.[25]
2. The mental and spiritual faculties that man has in common with God, such as intellectual and moral abilities, and original righteousness.
3. A physical resemblance, namely, that man looks like God.
4. Man rules on earth as God rules over the creation.
5. Man's ability to relate to God.[26]
6. Man's ability to create in an analogical fashion like God.

---

[24]Wenham, *Genesis*, p. 29; cf. Garr, *Image and Likeness*, pp. 95-115.

[25]Louth, *Genesis*, p. 29.

[26]Wenham, *Genesis*, p. 30. See 'Excursus: The History of the Exegesis of Gen. 1.26-27,' (Westerman, *Genesis*, pp. 147ff).

Of these six options, which one is the strongest? Is it even necessary to narrow one's choice to one option or is a holistic definition in order?

A holistic definition

Option 1 fails because it appeals to redeemed man when man has no need for redemption yet. Additionally, צֶלֶם (selem) and דְּמוּת (Dmût) are used interchangeably throughout Scripture.[27] Option 3 fails because Scripture teaches the incorporeality of God (Deut. 4:15-16).[28] It seems plausible, though, that God's image is a combination of options 2, 4, 5, and 6, with option 4 having primary emphasis. This combination appears to be the definition stated in verse 26b when God gives man dominion over the creation. One finds the image of God primarily in man's role as God's vice-regent over the creation, and secondarily in his mental and spiritual faculties, his ability to relate to God, and ability to create like God.[29] As Hoekema explains, the image of God in man must

> be seen as involving both the structure of man (his gifts, capacities, and endowments) and the functioning of man (his actions, his relationships to God and to others, and the way he uses his gifts). To stress either of these at the expense of the other is to be one-sided. ... To see man as the image of God is to see both the task and the gifts. But the task is primary; the gifts are secondary. The gifts are the means for fulfilling the task.[30]

---

[27]Sarna, *Genesis*, p. 12; Kidner, *Genesis*, pp. 50-51; Westermann, *Genesis*, p. 146; cf. Garr, *Image and Likeness*, p. 165.

[28]See Garr, *Image and Likness*, p. 131.

[29]Rabbinic interpreters primarily see the dominion of man in his ability to name the animals, a common ANE expression of sovereignty over something or someone (see *Mid. Rabb.* Gen. 17.4; see also G. K. Beale, 'Garden Temple,' *Kerux* 18/2 [2003], p. 6, n. 10).

[30]Hoekema, *Image of God*, p. 73.

This is basically the historical position within the Reformed tradition: God gave the man and woman 'living, reasonable and immortal souls; made them after his own image, in knowledge, righteousness, and holiness; having the law of God written in their hearts, and power to fulfill it, and dominion over the creatures; yet subject to fall' (WCF 1.17). In the same way that God has dominion over the cosmos, so too man, created in his image, has dominion over the earth.[31] This interpretation also makes sense against the background of the cosmogonies of the ancient Near East, the immediate historical backdrop for the Genesis narrative.

The image of God against the ancient Near East background

In Egypt and Mesopotamia the ruling monarch was described as the image or the likeness of a god. For example, one sees the monarch–divine image bearer connection in salutations found in ancient Near East literature:

> The father of my lord the king is the very image of Bel.
> The king, lord of the lands, is the image of Shamash.
> O king of the inhabited world, you are the image of Marduk.

Likewise, in Egypt the name Tutankhamen literally means 'the living image of the god Amun'.[32] G. K. Beale explains the connection between monarchs as the images of deities and explains that

> ancient kings would set up images of themselves in distant lands over which they ruled in order to represent their sovereign presence. For example, after conquering a

---

[31]Calvin, *Genesis*, p. 94; Sarna, *Genesis*, p. 12; Garr, *Image and Likeness*, pp. 155-56, 163.

[32]Sarna, *Genesis*, p. 12; see also Wenham, *Genesis*, p. 31.

new territory, the Assyrian king Shalmanesar 'fashioned a mighty image of my majesty' that he 'set up' on a black obelisk, and then he virtually equates his 'image' with that of 'the glory of Assur' his god. Likewise, Adam was created as the image of the divine king to indicate that earth was ruled over by Yahweh.[33]

So, then, against the backdrop of the literature of the ancient Near East we obtain a window through which we can capture some of the significance of man's creation in the image of God. The triune God created man in his image primarily to rule over the earth, endowing him with many other God-like qualities, to indicate that God ruled over the creation. He also created man in community, male and female, to reflect the divine community of the Trinity.

Yet, while there are similarities between ancient Near Eastern religious beliefs and the Genesis account at this point, there are significant differences. The ancient Near Eastern king bore the image of a god, but in the Genesis account mankind, male and female, bears God's image.[34] The ancient Israelite, knowing that Pharaoh claimed to bear the image of Re, the sun god, would read that all people bear the image of God. Moreover, a king was not to be worshiped as a demi-god, nor was man to be worshiped, because all are mere creatures.

The ancient Israelite would also know of God's attributes, and know that some of them were imparted to man in his creation. In the same way that God has attributes and abilities such as holiness, righteousness,

---

[33]G. K. Beale, 'Garden Temple,' p. 5; also Gerhard von Rad, *Old Testament Theology*, 2 vols. (1957; Louisville: Westminster John Knox, 2001), vol. 1, pp. 146-47. Beale also draws attention to the connection between the *imago Dei* and the responsibilities of man in the garden particularly as the Qumran community understood the relationship (see 4Q504-06, fr. 8; Garr, *Image and Likeness*, pp. 132, 135, 143-44).

[34]Wenham, *Genesis*, p. 31.

ability to create, and exercise of reason, so too man was given these attributes in their communicable form. John Calvin explains that man reflects God's attributes because the

> chief seat of the Divine image was in his mind and heart, where it was eminent. ... In the mind perfect intelligence flourished and reigned, uprightness attended as its companion, and all the senses were prepared and molded for due obedience to reason; and in the body there was a suitable correspondence with this internal order.[35]

Calvin's explanation is confirmed by God's blessing upon and approval of the newly created man (v. 28, 31), by man's exercise of reason in naming the animals (Gen. 2:19), and by procreation (Gen. 5:3). This interpretation seems to echo Psalm 8:3-6:

> When I consider your heavens, the work of your fingers, the moon and the stars, which you have ordained, what is man that you are mindful of him, and the son of man that you visit him? For you have made him a little lower than the angels, and you have crowned him with glory and honor. You have made him to have dominion over the works of your hands; you have put all things under his feet.

Set against the ancient Near Eastern religions in which the 'forces of nature are divinities that may hold the human race in thralldom, our text declares man to be a free agent who has the God-given power to control nature.'[36] Moreover, no man or any other creature is a deity. Rather, God's image, his communicable attributes, were given to man so he could rule as God's vicegerent over the creation.[37]

---

[35]Calvin, *Genesis*, p. 93.

[36]Sarna, *Genesis*, p. 13.

[37]See DSS 1QS, ln. 17-18. Also, Wolhart Pannenberg, *Systematic*

Man: the apex of creation

In Genesis 1:27 one reads that 'God created man in his own image, in the image of God he created him; male and female he created them.' Two features of this verse stand out: (1) the use of the verb ברא (br'), and (2) the image of God as both man and woman.

First, the author uses the verb ברא (br') three times in this one verse. This repetition most likely indicates the superlative, namely, that man is the apex of God's creation. As Herman Bavinck comments: 'Among creatures, only man is the image of God, God's highest and richest self-revelation and consequently the head and crown of the whole creation, the *imago Dei* and the epitome of nature, both *mikrotheos* (microgod) and *mikrokosmos* (microcosm).'[38]

Second, God creates man as male and female. According to early rabbinic interpreters, man was created with two faces; he was a hermaphrodite.[39] This teaching, however, runs contrary to Scripture, especially to biblical teaching about marriage. Why, if man was originally a hermaphrodite, would there be any need for woman? Why did not man reproduce asexually? The male sex does not alone possess the image of God. Man, as male and female, bears the image of God, the apex of the creation.[40]

Summary

Thus far the exegetical data has shown that the triune God created man, male and female, in his image. That God created man in his image and placed him in the world to rule over the creation was a declaration that

---

Theology, vol. 2, trans. G. W. Bromiley (Grand Rapids: Eerdmans, 1994), p. 203.

[38]Herman Bavinck, *Reformed Dogmatics*, vol. 2, *God and Creation*, trans. John Vriend, ed. John Bolt (Grand Rapids: Baker, 2004), p. 531.

[39]Cassuto, *Genesis*, p. 57; *Mid. Rabb.* Gen. 8.1.

[40]Sarna, *Genesis*, p. 13.

the triune God ruled over the creation. Additionally, the evidence shows that man possessed many of the qualities of God, reflecting his communicable attributes. As the introduction to this chapter stated, however, one cannot stop with this information believing that one has defined the image of God. Though man was created in the image of God, he was not created in an indefectible state – man fell from his exalted position necessitating his redemption. As Hoekema writes, 'The integrity in which Adam and Eve existed before the Fall was not a state of consummate and unchangeable perfection.'[41] In order to define completely the image of God, one must turn to Christ, the uncreated image of God.

Christ the image of God

What any study of the man created in the image of God must include is the acknowledgment that Christ is the image of God. Christ as the image of God has two important doctrinal points: (1) the image of Christ defines what man truly is supposed to be; and (2) it governs the goal of man's redemption. First, that Christ is the perfect image of God is attested in a number of places throughout the New Testament (2 Cor. 4:4; Col. 1:15; Heb. 1:3). This means that Christ is the perfect man. Or, to state the idea in technical terms, christology defines anthropology. Irenaeus long ago saw the defining nature of christology vis-à-vis anthropology: 'When, however, the Word of God became flesh, He confirmed both these: for He both showed forth the image truly, since He became Himself what was His image; and He re-established the similitude after a sure manner, by assimilating man to the invisible Father through means of the visible Word.'[42] One cannot know what it means to bear the image of God apart from the incarnation of Christ.[43] This does not mean that Adam and Christ are the image of God in the same manner.

---

[41]Hoekema, *Image of God*, p. 83.
[42]Irenaeus, *Against Heresies*, 5.16.4, in *ANF*, vol. 1, p. 544.

Bavinck concisely explains the differences between the first and second Adam, Jesus Christ:

> Like the Son, so also man as such is altogether the image of God. He does not just bear but *is* the image of God. There is this difference, of course, that what the Son is in an absolute sense, man is in only a relative sense. The former is the eternal only begotten Son; the latter is the created son of God. The former is the image of God *within* the divine being, the latter *outside* of it. The one is the image of God in a divine manner, the other is that in a creaturely manner.[44]

Keeping these differences in mind, the rest of the study will demonstrate how Christ, the second Adam, images God perfectly by being obedient to the will of his heavenly Father. Christ images God by exercising dominion over the creation, indicating that indeed the triune God does rule the creation, something that the first Adam failed to do. As Hoekema writes, one 'must learn to know what the image of God is by looking at Jesus Christ.'[45]

Second, Christ as the image of God governs the goal of man's redemption. Yes, man was created in the image of God but due to the fall the image has been marred by sin. Concerning the damage of sin upon the image of God in man, Calvin observes, 'There is no doubt that Adam, when he fell from his state, was by this defection alienated from God. Therefore, even though we grant that God's image was not totally annihilated and destroyed in him, yet it was so corrupted that whatever remains is frightful deformity.'[46] The New Testament states in several places that those whom God 'foreknew he also predestined to be conformed to the image of

---

[43]Pannenberg, *Systematic Theology*, p. 208.

[44]Bavinck, *Reformed Dogmatics*, p. 533.

[45]Hoekema, *Image of God*, p. 22.

[46]John Calvin, *Institutes of the Christian Religion*, LCC, vols. 20-21, ed. John T. McNeill, trans. Ford Lewis Battles (Philadelphia: Westminster, 1960), 1.15.4, p. 189.

his Son' (Rom. 8:29; cf. 2 Cor. 3:18). Paul writes of the relationship between those that bear the image of the first and last Adams: 'As was the man of dust, so also are those who are of the dust, and as is the man of heaven, so also are those who are of heaven. Just as we have borne the image of the man of dust, we shall also bear the image of the man of heaven' (1 Cor. 15:48-49). Again, as Hoekema comments: 'Since Christ is God's perfect image, likeness to Christ will also mean likeness to God. This perfect likeness to Christ and to God is the ultimate goal of our sanctification.'[47] Likewise, Calvin observes: 'The beginning of our recovery of salvation is in that restoration which we obtain through Christ, who also is called the Second Adam for the reason that he restores us to the true and complete integrity.'[48] So, then, when considering that man is the image of God, one must keep Christ in the foreground.

Conclusion

Man, male and female, was created in the image of God, reflecting both the unity and community of the Trinity. He was placed in the creation to rule as God's vicegerent, a claim upon the creation of God's sovereignty and rule over the cosmos. Adam was to exercise dominion over the creation and was endowed with many gifts, abilities, and God-like qualities. Bavinck notes that

> Thus man forms a unity of the material and spiritual world, a mirror of the universe, a connecting link, compendium, the epitome of all nature, a microcosm, and, precisely on that account, also the image and likeness of God, his son and heir, a micro-divine-being (*mikrotheos*). He is the prophet who explains God and proclaims his excellencies; he is the priest who consecrates himself with all that is created to God as a holy offering; he is the king who governs all things in

---

[47]Hoekema, *Image of God*, p. 31.
[48]Calvin, *Institutes*, 1.15.4, p. 189.

justice and rectitude. And in all this he points to One who in a still higher and richer sense is the revelation and image of God, to him who is the only begotten of the Father, and the firstborn of all creatures. Adam, the son of God, was a type of Christ.[49]

Adam, then, was the first prophet, priest, and king. Adam rebelled against his creator and Father, necessitating his redemption by a second Adam, one who also bears the image of God. The second Adam, however, was unlike the first Adam. It is ultimately the differences between the first and second Adams that Genesis 1–3 sets to demonstrate, and these will dominate the sub-sequent chapters in this study. To explore the similarities and differences between the two Adams, the two image bearers of God, one must turn to the garden itself to examine the setting in which the first Adam was placed.

---

[49]Bavinck, *Reformed Dogmatics*, p. 562.

2

THE GARDEN-TEMPLE OF EDEN

Introduction
When one comes to the narrative of Genesis 2, interpreters typically identify the garden of Eden as a
Mesopotamian farm, whose responsibility to tend
was Adam's. For example, Henry Morris writes that
'Adam was instructed merely to till the ground in the
Garden of Eden, to dress it and keep it'. Commenting
on Genesis 2:15, John Calvin similarly writes that 'the
earth was given to man, with this condition, that he
should occupy himself in its cultivation'. Martin Luther
maintains that Adam received a twofold duty, 'to work
or cultivate this garden and, furthermore, to watch and
guard it.' Gerhard von Rad supports this interpretation
with evidence from the practices of the ancient Near East
and states that 'the cultivation of vegetable gardens was
widely practiced in the ancient Orient'.[1]

Is this the intent of the passage? Is Adam merely
a farmer? From Genesis 2, is the reader supposed to
extrapolate a work-ethic? Quite simply, No. If the garden

---

[1]Henry Morris, *The Genesis Record: A Scientific and Devotional
Commentary on the Book of Beginnings* (Grand Rapids: Baker,
1976), p. 92; John Calvin, *Commentary on Genesis*, CTS, trans.
James Anderson (1849; Grand Rapids: Baker, 1993), p. 125; Martin
Luther, *Lectures on Genesis*, LW, vol. 1, ed. Jaroslav Pelikan (St.
Louis: Concordia, 1958), p. 102; Gerhard von Rad, *Genesis*, OTL
(1961; Philadelphia: Westminster, 1972), p. 77.

is merely a farm, then one might logically extrapolate a work-ethic; but if it is the earthly archetypal temple, then the nature of the work is of an entirely different order. In other words, is Adam's responsibility farming or are his duties priestly? There is data, not only within the Genesis narrative but in other portions of Scripture, that lead to the conclusion that the garden is the archetypal earthly temple. The investigation must therefore proceed to an examination of the evidence to see why the garden must be recognized as the first temple. This chapter will proceed by first examining the features of the garden and second the activity of its inhabitants.

The features of the garden

Eastern location

Genesis 2:8 states that God planted the garden in the east. There are a handful of passages in the prophecy of Ezekiel that give the east special significance in connection with God's presence. Ezekiel is brought to the eastern gate on the east side of the temple (Ezek. 11:1) and watches the glory of the Lord depart over the Mount of Olives towards the east (Ezek. 11:23). Twenty years later Ezekiel saw the glory of the Lord return through the eastern gate (Ezek. 43:1-4) and it was shut and was to remain closed because 'the LORD, the God of Israel, has entered by it' (Ezek. 44:1-2).[2] During the time of the Herodian temple, the eastern gate was used only by the high priest and those helping him lead the sacrificial heifer to the Mount of Olives (Middot 1.3).[3] In addition to the ingress and egress of the glory of the Lord from the east, there is also the imagery of the sun, which rises in the east, a favorite biblical metaphor for divine revelation (Luke 1:78-79).

---

[2]The Qumran community also identified the east as the direction of blessing because that was the location of paradise, or the garden (4Q206 1 26 [1 En. 32.1-3]).

[3]Cleon L. Rogers, 'קָדִים,' in NIDOTTE, vol. 3, pp. 871-72.

On a mountain top

When one examines Genesis 1–3, there is no explicit statement that the garden of Eden sits atop a mountain. There is indirect evidence, however, that shows that the garden sits at a higher elevation than the rest of the surrounding topography. The raised elevation of the garden is evident because Genesis 2:10-14 states that a river flowed out of Eden. Water flows downstream, from higher to lower elevations. Further evidence emerges in the prophet Ezekiel, who pronounces a judgment against the king of Tyre and incorporates imagery from the garden: 'You were on the holy mountain of God' (Ezek. 28:14), and 'I cast you as a profane thing from the mountain of God' (v. 16). Ezekiel identifies the location of the garden of Eden on the mountain of God.[4] Fanning out into the rest of Scripture, one finds that God dwells atop mountains: Horeb (Exod. 3:1) or Sinai (Exod. 18:5; 24:13), and Zion (Ps. 48:1-2). The New Testament authors continue this theme and identify the eschatological dwelling-place of God and his people as a mountain top: 'But you have come to Mount Zion and to the city of the living God, the heavenly Jerusalem' (Heb. 12:22). Similar imagery appears in John's apocalypse: 'And he carried me away in the Spirit to a great, high mountain, and showed me the holy city Jerusalem coming down out of heaven from God' (Rev. 21:10; cf. 14:1). Scripture makes an important connection between the presence of God in the temple and the temple's location atop mountains. The fact that the river flowed from Eden and the statements from Ezekiel confirm that the garden of Eden sat atop a mountain.

The river of Eden

Genesis 2:10 states that 'A river flowed out of Eden to water the garden'. While within the original context

---

[4]Cf. Daniel I. Block, *The Book of Ezekiel: Chapters 25-48*, NICOT (Grand Rapids: Eerdmans, 1998), p. 114; Walther Zimmerli, *Ezekiel 2*, trans. James D. Martin (Philadelphia: Fortress, 1983), pp. 92-93.

the river serves the purpose of providing the garden
with some of the necessary irrigation for the growth
of vegetation, there are undoubtedly connections between this river and subsequent temple imagery in the
Bible. Water, of course, is a powerful symbol of life
throughout Scripture and one often connected with
divine sanctuaries.[5] Scripture makes this river-temple
connection, for example, in Psalm 46:4: 'There is a
river whose streams make glad the city of God, the holy
habitation of the Most High.' A river also flows out from
under the threshold of the temple in Ezekiel's temple
vision (Ezek. 47:1)[6] and heals anything with which it
comes into contact (Ezek. 47:8). The temple in Jerusalem
was the center of God's presence, though some scholars
speculate whether there was a literal spring or source of
water under the temple mount.[7] The river imagery found
in Ezekiel's vision should be understood, however, to be
symbolic.

Confirmation that the references to water and rivers
are symbolic imagery can be found in a number of places
throughout Scripture. Jeremiah calls God, 'the fountain
of living waters' (Jer. 2:13), while in a similar vein
God's revelation is connected to the symbolic imagery
of a river in the prophet Isaiah; God's prophetic word
is compared to 'The waters of Shiloah that flow softly'
(Isa. 8:6). Because the people reject God's word, 'the
Lord is bringing up against them the waters of the River,
mighty and many' (Isa. 8:7). There is also river imagery
tied to the temple of God in the prophets Zechariah and

---

[5]Gordon J. Wenham, 'Sanctuary Symbolism in the Garden of
Eden Story,' in *I Studied Inscriptions from Before the Flood: Ancient
Near Eastern, Literary, and Linguistic Approaches to Genesis 1-11*,
eds. Richard S. Hess and David Toshio Tsumura, Sources for Biblical
and Theological Study, vol. 4 (Winona Lake: Eisenbrauns, 1994),
p. 402; idem, *Proceedings of the Ninth World Congress of Jewish
Studies, Division A: The Period of the Bible* (Jerusalem: World Union
of Jewish Studies, 1986), pp. 19-25.

[6]Block, *Ezekiel*, p. 691.

[7]Zimmerli, *Ezekiel*, p. 510.

Joel: 'A fountain shall come forth from the house of the LORD' (Joel 3:18; cf. Zech. 14:8). Of course one finds in John's apocalypse the most powerful imagery in the connection between the temple of God and a river: 'Then the angel showed me the river of the water of life, bright as crystal, flowing from the throne of God and of the Lamb' (Rev. 22:1). This river-temple imagery points in several directions.

First, while one must recognize the connection between the imagery of water and the presence of God, it is especially relevant when pertaining to the Holy Spirit: 'Whoever believes in me, as the Scripture has said, "Out of his heart will flow rivers of living water." Now this he said about the Spirit' (John 7:38-39a).[8] Second, water and river imagery is connected with the idea of God's divine word, which produces belief in the heart of man when proclaimed in conjunction with the work of the Holy Spirit. These two attributions, however, are closely associated with the presence of God and his dwelling place, namely the temple. For these reasons Meredith Kline rightly concludes that God's presence on his 'mountain throne-site in Eden was evidently the spring-source of the river in paradise'.[9]

The trees of the garden

Most people are aware of the garden's two famous trees, the tree of life and the tree of knowledge (Gen. 2:9). There are connections between the garden and the temple accoutrements in the description of the tree of knowledge. Genesis 3:6 describes the fruit of this tree as 'good for food, a delight to the eyes, and desired to make

---

[8]G. K. Beale, *The Book of Revelation*, NIGTC (Grand Rapids: Eerdmans, 1999), p. 1104.

[9]Meredith G. Kline, *Images of the Spirit* (Eugene: Wipf & Stock, 1998), p. 42. This idea is repeated in the Qumran community, which believed that the earth would be filled with priests who would drink water which flowed out from under the walls of the city (4Q537). Similar imagery appears in *The Testament of Levi* (*ANF*, vol. 8, § 18, p. 16).

one wise.' The psalmist echoes this description when he writes about the law of God: the law of God makes the simple wise, rejoices the heart, and enlightens the eyes (Ps. 19:8-9).[10] The Decalogue, a copy of the law, was kept inside the ark in the holy of holies, with the book of the law beside it (Exod. 25:16; Deut. 31:26). The Israelites knew that to touch the ark or see it uncovered brought certain death, as did eating from the tree of knowledge (2 Sam. 6:7; Num. 4:20).[11] There appears to be a connection, then, between the tree of knowledge as a visible representation of God's law and the psalmist's description of the law of God. The law of God is always present in some form in God's temple, whether the tree of knowledge as a visible representation of God's command, or the presence of the law within the ark.

This, however, is not the only connection between the trees of the garden and the temple. There is a further connection between the tree of life and the temple menorah. God instructed Moses to craft the menorah, or lamp stand, which was essentially a golden tree with branches, buds, and almond flowers (Exod. 25:31-39). The menorah, scholars argue, refers back to the tree of life in the garden.[12] If one takes a clue from the architecture of the tabernacle and temple, the menorah was in relatively close proximity to the holy of holies, the throne of God. Interestingly enough, Jewish literature places the tree of life near the throne of God in the garden of Eden: 'The throne of God was made ready where the tree of life was.'[13]

---

[10]D. J. A. Clines, 'The Tree of Knowledge and the Law of Yahweh,' *VT* 24 (1974), pp. 8-14.

[11]Wenham, 'Sanctuary Symbolism,' pp. 402-03.

[12]Wenham, 'Sanctuary Symbolism,' p. 401; and Vern S. Poythress, *The Shadow of Christ in the Law of Moses* (Phillipsburg: P & R, 1991), p. 19; G. K. Beale, *The Temple and the Church's Mission: A Biblical Theology of the Dwelling Place of God*, NSBT, vol. 17 (Downers Grove: InterVarsity, 2004), p. 71. Rabbinic interpreters, however, connect the tree of life with the Torah (*Mid. Rabb.* Deut. 1.1).

[13]*Revelation of Moses*, ANF, vol. 8, p. 567. See also James D. G.

Beyond the Genesis narrative (2:8-9), one finds that there were many different kinds of trees in the garden: 'The cedars in the garden of God could not rival it, nor the fir trees equal its boughs; neither were the plane trees like its branches; no tree in the garden of God was its equal in beauty. I made it beautiful in the mass of its branches, and all the trees of Eden envied it, that were in the garden of God' (Ezek. 31:8-9). The plentitude of trees is reflected in the architecture of the temple. The decorative features of the temple included carvings of flowers, pomegranates, and palm trees (1 Kings 6:18, 29, 32; 7:18ff).[14] Besides the Solomonic temple, trees are also a part of Ezekiel's vision of the eschatological temple (Ezek. 41:18-26; 47:12). Palm trees appear, which are most likely symbolic of life and prosperity, certainly a characteristic of life in the garden.[15]

Trees in connection with the temple make their most prominent appearance in John's apocalypse, where the tree of life appears for the first time since being mentioned in the opening Genesis narrative: 'On either side of the river was the tree of life, bearing twelve kinds of fruit, yielding its fruit every month; and the leaves of the tree were for the healing of the nations' (Rev. 22:2, 14; NASB; cf. Ezek. 47:12).

Dunn, *The Theology of Paul the Apostle* (Grand Rapids: Eerdmans, 1998), p. 88.

[14]Kline, *Images of the Spirit*, p. 41. Rabbinic interpreters state that Solomon decorated the temple with all sorts of trees made out of gold (*Mid. Rabb.* Songs 3.22).

[15]Block, *Ezekiel*, p. 558. There is a possible connection between the palm trees that adorn the temple and the use of palm fronds in the triumphal entry of Christ to Jerusalem (John 12:13). There are hints of this connection from the intertestamental history of Israel. Simon the Maccabee drove Syrian forces out of Jerusalem waving palm branches (1 Macc. 13.51), and they were also used in the rededication of the temple (2 Macc. 10.6). Likewise, apocalyptic visions of the end of history utilize palm branches: 'And when Levi became as a sun, a certain young man gave to him twelve branches of palm' (*Testament of Naphtali*, §5, cf. §8 in *ANF*, v. 8, p. 28; also see D. A. Carson, *The Gospel According to John* [Grand Rapids: Eerdmans, 1991], p. 28).

Similarly, Ezekiel sees a river that flows 'from the sanctuary', which causes 'trees for food' to grow on both banks of the river; Ezekiel states: 'Their fruit will be for food, and their leaves for healing' (Ezek. 47:12).[16] John sees virtually the same picture, 'the river of the water of life' proceeding 'from the throne of God and of the Lamb' (Rev. 22:1). On either side of the river John sees the tree of life, and that 'the leaves of the tree were for the healing of the nations' (Rev. 22:2). These passages contain clear connections between the trees of the garden and the subsequent temples, but especially with the tree of life, as it reappears in both Ezekiel and John's apocalypse.[17]

The precious stones and metal
Genesis 2:10-14 records the presence of precious stones and metals: gold and onyx. Rabbinic interpreters argue that the reason God created gold was so that it could be used for the temple (*Mid. Rabb.* Gen. 16:2). In Ezekiel's prophecy against the king of Tyre there are many other types of precious stones and metal that appear in the garden: sardius, topaz, diamonds, beryl, onyx, jasper,

---

[16]For similar eschatological imagery in the Qumran community, especially as it concerns the consumption of fruit only by priests, see 4Q266, fr. 6; 4Q396-7.

[17]Beale, *Revelation*, p. 1107. We should not pass by the connection between the temple and the Church. New Testament scholarship is largely united in the idea that the Church is the eschatological temple of God (1 Cor. 6:19; Eph. 2:21; 1 Pet. 2:5). If the garden is a temple, then in what way does the garden typify the Church? The answer is to be found in the presence of the trees of the garden. It is the garden of Eden as a temple and therefore a type of the Church that gives us the contextual background for the OT imagery of the righteous being 'like a tree planted by streams of water that yields its fruit in its season, and its leaf does not wither' (Ps. 1:3). The tree–Church connection appears to also inform the New Testament imagery to the same effect (Matt. 3.10; 7.17-20; Gal. 5.22; cf. John 15.1ff). Just as the first Adam stood in the midst of a host of fruit bearing trees, so too the second Adam will stand in the midst of the throng of saints, described by Scripture as fruit-bearing trees.

sapphires, emeralds, carbuncle, and gold (Ezek. 28:13). Once again, exploring the rest of Scripture one finds that the bulk of the sacred items of the tabernacle furniture were made of or covered with pure gold (Exod. 25:11, 17, 24, 29, 36).[18] Some of the precious stones that were in the garden reappear in the high priest's vestments, specifically his breast–piece: sardius, topaz, carbuncle, emerald, sapphire, diamond, jacinth, agate, amethyst, beryl, onyx, and jasper. All of these precious stones were placed in gold settings (Exod. 28:17-20).[19] The high priest's breast-piece was supposed to be 'a small replica of the earthly tabernacle, which itself was modeled on the heavenly tabernacle.'[20] It should be no surprise, then, to find these same precious stones, or their semantic equivalents, reappearing in the foundation of the eschatological temple in John's apocalypse. John is carried away to the 'high mountain' (Rev. 21:10) where he examines the twelve foundations of the holy city and finds jasper, sapphire, agate, emerald, onyx, carnelian, chrysolite, beryl, topaz, chrysoprase, jacinth, and amethyst (Rev. 21:18-20).[21]

The cherubim

After man's fall and subsequent ejection from the garden God posted two cherubim outside the east entrance of the garden (Gen. 3:24). Throughout the Scriptures, the cherubim are the guardians of God's temples. In Solomon's temple two cherubim guard the inner sanctuary (1 Kings 6:23-28). Two cherubim sit atop the ark of the covenant, which forms the throne of God in the inner sanctuary (Exod. 25:18-22). There are also depictions of two cherubim decorating the curtains of

---

[18]Wenham, 'Sanctuary Symbolism,' p. 402.

[19]Wenham, 'Sanctuary Symbolism,' p. 402.

[20]Beale, *Revelation*, p. 1080.

[21]Beale, *Revelation*, p. 1081; Kline, *Images of the Spirit*, pp. 42-47; also Alfred Edersheim, *The Temple: Its Ministry and Services As They Were at the Time of Jesus Christ* (Grand Rapids: Kregel, 1997), p. 72.

the tabernacle and the walls of the temple (Exod. 26:31; 1 Kings 6:29).[22] This information provides the reader with data concerning the placement and movement of the cherubim, which have important implications not only for the identity of the garden as a temple, but also for redemptive history and christology.

In Ezekiel's prophecy against the king of Tyre, the king is compared to a cherub in the garden: 'You were an anointed guardian cherub. I placed you; you were on the holy mountain of God; in the midst of the stones of fire you walked' (Ezek. 28:14). The cherub, who is in the presence of God, walks back and forth in the garden.[23] Ezekiel's description is ostensibly a similar station and function to that of the cherubim that surround the throne of God in John's apocalypse (Rev. 4:6-8). Now, it is important that, while the cherubim first appear in the garden, subsequent to man's fall they are moved to the eastern entrance (Gen. 3:24). The cherubim that guard the entrance to the garden, the place of God's presence, are symbolically reproduced on the curtain that God instructs Moses to hang between the inner sanctuary and the holy of holies (Exod. 26:33). The Genesis narrative, then, appears to identify the garden as the holy of holies, in which man had direct access to God's presence. Subsequent to the fall, God moved the cherubim to the outer perimeter of the holy of holies to keep man from entering.[24] Just as the cherubim with the flaming sword would ostensibly slay anyone who tried to gain access, so too anyone who attempted to enter the holy of holies in the tabernacle or temple would be struck down. Only the high priest, and then only once a year on the day of atonement, and only according to

---

[22]Wenham, 'Sanctuary Symbolism,' p. 401.

[23]Block, *Ezekiel*, p. 113.

[24]Poythress, *Shadow of Christ*, p. 19; similarly Karl Barth, *Church Dogmatics*, vol. 3.1, trans. J. W. Edwards (1958; Edinburgh: T & T Clark, 1998), p. 254.

God's prescriptions (Lev. 16:2ff), could safely enter into the most holy place.

The redemptive-historical and christological connections are clearly spelled out in the New Testament – it is Christ who tears away the veil (Matt. 27:51), essentially moving the cherubim from their station on the outer perimeter of the holy of holies and returning them to their place before God's throne. Man may once again, through Christ, approach God in the holy of holies (Heb. 9:24-25). More will be written about the connection between Adam and Christ in the chapter on the second Adam; but, for now, suffice it to say that the presence of the cherubim is another piece of evidence that confirms the garden is a temple. At this point, we shall proceed to examine the activity of both God and man within the garden, to search for further corroborating evidence that supports the thesis that the garden is a temple.

Activity of the inhabitants

God's presence
Regarding the activity of the inhabitants of the garden, there is the language used to describe God's presence; it is the same as that found in passages describing God's activity in subsequent temple appearances. God was 'walking in the garden' (Gen. 3:8). The Old Testament states, for example: 'I will make my dwelling [lit. tabernacle] among you. ... I will walk among you' (Lev. 26:11-12; cf. Deut. 23:14). 'I have not lived in a house since the day I brought up the people of Israel from Egypt to this day, but I have been moving about [lit. walked] in a tent for my dwelling' (2 Sam. 7:6). So, as Gordon Wenham notes, 'the Lord walked in Eden as he subsequently walked in the tabernacle.'[25]

---

[25]Wenham, 'Sanctuary Symbolism,' p. 401. The Qumran community makes the same connections between the presence of the Lord and his ambulatory activity (4Q504-6 fr. 6; fr. 8 recto).

God's creation of the garden

Yet another parallel between the garden and subsequent temples is evident in the creation of the garden and the construction of the desert tabernacle. Scholars have noted the parallel between the seven days of creation (Gen. 1:1–2:3) and the seven speeches of God to Moses providing instructions for the building of the tabernacle. The speeches give explicit directions concerning the materials (Exod. 25:1-9), ark (25:10-22), table (25:23-30), lampstand (25:31-40), tabernacle (26:1-37), bronze altar (27:1-8), and the courtyard (27:9-19).[26]

Wenham also notes that there are 'parallels in phraseology between the conclusion of the creation account in 1:1–2:3 and the tabernacle building account in Exodus 25–40.'[27] At the end of God's creative activity, he rests on the seventh day (Gen. 2:2-3). Likewise, when God finished the seventh speech to Moses he prescribed the Sabbath rest (Exod. 31:17), and when Moses finished constructing the temple God's presence in 'the cloud rested above it, and the glory of the LORD filled the tabernacle' (Exod. 40:35, NKJV).[28] God rests

---

[26]Wenham, 'Sanctuary Symbolism,' p. 403; David A. Dorsey, *The Literary Structure of the Old Testament: A Commentary on Genesis-Malachi* (Grand Rapids: Baker Books, 1999), p. 75; cf. John I. Durham, *Exodus*, WBC, vol. 3 (Dallas: Word, 1987), p. 473. Interestingly enough, Weinfeld notes that Moses had to wait six days at the foot of Sinai before climbing the mountain to receive the instructions for the tabernacle, which perhaps correspond to the six days of creation (Exod. 24:15ff). Similarly, Christ also ascended the mount of transfiguration after six days (Mark 9:2; Matt. 17:1) (Moshe Weinfeld, 'Sabbath, Temple and the Enthronement of the Lord,' in *Mélanges Bibliques et Orientaux en l'honneur de M. Henri Cazelles*, eds. A. Caquot et M. Delcor [Neukirchen-Vluyn: NeukirchenerVerlag, 1981], p. 506).

[27]Wenham, 'Sanctuary Symbolism,' p. 403; also Peter J. Kearney, 'Creation and Liturgy: The P Redaction of Ex 25-40,' *ZAW* 89 (1977), p. 375-78; Joseph Blenkinsopp, *Prophecy and Canon* (Notre Dame: University of Notre Dame Press, 1977), p. 62; cf. Weinfeld, 'Sabbath, Temple and the Enthronement,' p. 502, n. 5.

[28]Kearney, 'Creation and Liturgy,' p. 378; also Weinfeld, 'Sabbath, Temple and the Enthronement,' p. 501.

once the creation is finished in the garden-temple and likewise rests in the newly finished holy of holies in the wilderness tabernacle.

These are not new observations but have precedence in rabbinic interpretation. Rabbinic interpreters make the following connections between the construction of the tabernacle and the creation week:

The expression, *the tabernacle*, denotes that its importance was equal to that of the world, which is called 'tent,' even as the tabernacle is called 'tent.' How can this statement be supported? It is written, 'In the beginning God created the heaven' (Gen. 1:1), and it is written, 'Who stretches out the heaven like a curtain' (Ps. 104:2), while of the tabernacle it is written, 'And you shall make curtains of goat's hair for a tent over the tabernacle' (Exod. 26:7). It is written in connection with the second day, 'Let there be a firmament ... and let it divide' (Gen. 1:6), and of the tabernacle it is written, 'The veil shall divide unto you' (Exod. 26.33). Of the third day we read, 'Let the waters under the heaven be gathered together' (Gen. 1:9), and of the tabernacle it is written, 'You shall also make a laver of brass, and the base thereof of brass, whereat to wash' (Exod. 30:18). Of the fourth day, 'Let there be lights in the firmament of the heaven' (Gen. 1:14), and of the tabernacle, 'You shall make a candlestick of pure gold' (Exod. 25:31). Of the fifth, 'Let fowl fly above the earth' (Gen. 1:20), and of the tabernacle, 'The cherubim shall spread out their wings' (Exod. 25:20). On the sixth day man was created, and in connection with the tabernacle it says, 'Bring near unto you Aaron your brother' (Exod. 28:1). Of the seventh day we have it written, 'and the heaven and the earth were finished' (Gen. 2:1), and of the tabernacle, 'Thus was finished all the work of the tabernacle' (Exod. 39:32). In connection with the creation of the world it is written, 'And God blessed' (Gen. 2.3), and in connection with the tabernacle, 'And Moses blessed them' (Exod. 39:43). On the seventh day God finished (Gen. 2.2), and in connection with the tabernacle, 'It

69

came to pass on the day that Moses had made an end.' On the seventh day he hallowed it (Gen. 2:3), and in connection with the tabernacle he 'sanctified it' (7:1). Thus we have explained the expression *the tabernacle* (*Mid. Rabb.* Num. 12:13).[29]

In other words, the tabernacle, which was a temple, was a microcosmic reproduction of God's cosmic temple, the creation.[30] The relationship between the creation and the tabernacle is more clearly seen in the following chart:

Day	Creation	Tabernacle
Day 1	Heavens are stretched out like a curtain (Ps. 104:2)	Tent (Exod. 26:7)
Day 2	Firmament (Gen. 1:2)	Temple veil (Exod. 26:33)
Day 3	Waters below firmament	Laver or bronze sea (Exod. 30:18)
Day 4	Lights (Gen. 1:14)	Light stand (Exod. 25:31)
Day 5	Birds (Gen. 1:20)	Winged cherubim (Exod. 25:20)
Day 6	Man (Gen. 1:27)	Aaron the high priest (Exod. 28:1)
Day 7	Cessation (Gen. 2:1)	Cessation (Exod. 39:32)
	Blessing (Gen. 2:3)	Mosaic blessing (Exod. 39:43)
	Completion (Gen. 2:2)	Completion (Exod. 39:43)

---

[29]Along similar lines Josephus remarks that the tabernacle was 'made in way of imitation and representation of the universe' (Antiquities 3.180, in *Works*, trans. William Whitson [Peabody: Hendrickson, 1987]).

[30]Beale, *Temple*, pp. 31-38.

The tabernacle–creation parallels mean that, if the creation is part of God's cosmic temple, then the garden of Eden was the first holy of holies, the location of God's throne. Moreover, Adam is the first priest. Adam's responsibilities further corroborate this conclusion.

Adam's responsibilities

To what end did God, after he had created Adam, put him in the garden? He placed him in the garden 'to work it and keep it' (Gen. 2:15). As previously noted, many commentators cast this labor in terms of the cultivation of agriculture, farming. Yet, the same vocabulary – 'work,' עבד ('vd) and 'keep' שמר (šmr) – is used to describe the priestly responsibilities in the tabernacle: 'They shall keep guard [שמר / šmr] over him ... before the tent of meeting, as they minister [עבד / 'vd] at the tabernacle' (Num. 3:7-8; cf. 4:23-24, 26).[31] Wenham notes that

> midrash drew attention to passages where these terms were used separately. It did not note though that the only other passages in the Pentateuch where these verbs are used together are to be found in Num. 3:7-8, 8:26, 18:5-6, of the Levites' duties in guarding and ministering in the sanctuary. If Eden is seen then as an ideal sanctuary, then perhaps Adam should be described as an archetypal Levite.[32]

Read within the greater context of Scripture, Adam's responsibilities in the garden are primarily priestly rather than agricultural.[33]

---

[31]Kline, *Images of the Spirit*, p. 35; Beale, *Temple*, pp. 66-70.

[32]Wenham, 'Sanctuary Symbolism,' p. 401; similarly Barth, *Dogmatics*, vol. 3.1, p. 254; Meredith G. Kline, *Kingdom Prologue: Genesis Foundations for a Covenantal Worldview* (Overland Park: Two Age Press, 2000), p. 88.

[33]Contra Victor P. Hamilton, *Handbook on the Pentateuch* (Grand Rapids: Baker, 1982), p. 52.

Adam's post-fall vestments

As we consider the priestly vestments of the Levites, we should note that specific terminology was used to describe the investiture of kings and priests, i.e. the hiphil form of the verb לבש (lvš). The hiphil 'can denote the causing of an event in which a person or object is esteemed or declared through a juridical sentence or some kind of recognition to be in a state.'[34] In other words, the investiture of the Levitical priests was akin to their installment to office, which is reflected with the use of the hiphil stem.

This can be seen, for example, in the following: 'Pharaoh ... clothed him in garments of fine linen' (Gen. 41:42); 'Put on Aaron the holy garments. And you shall anoint him and consecrate him, that he may serve me as priest' (Exod. 40:13; cf. 28:41; 29:8); 'And Moses brought Aaron's sons and clothed them with coats' (Lev. 8:13); 'Then Saul clothed David with his armor ... and clothed him with a coat of mail' (1 Sam. 17:38). לבש (lvš) is the same verb that is used when God clothed Adam and Eve: 'The LORD God made for Adam and for his wife garments of skins and clothed them' (Gen. 3:21). While Adam and Eve's clothing points forward to the covering that God provides his people in the righteousness of Christ, one should not miss the parallels between the dressing of man in Eden and the subsequent investiture of the temple priests.[35]

---

[34]Bruce K. Waltke and M. O' Connor, *An Introduction to Biblical Hebrew Syntax* (Winona Lake: Eisenbrauns, 1990), p. 439.

[35]Rabbinic interpreters identify Adam's vestments as those of a high priest. It was the firstborn that performed sacrifices. They state: 'Go back to the beginning of the creation of the world. Adam was the world's firstborn. When he offered his sacrifice, as it says: 'And it pleased the Lord better than a bullock that hath horns and hoofs' (Ps. 69:32) – he donned high priestly garments; as it says: 'And the Lord God made for Adam and for his wife garments of skins, and clothed them' (Gen. 3:21)' (*Mid. Rabb.* Num. 4.8).

One can further illuminate the parallel between the clothing of kings, but especially that of priests, when he considers that priests were not allowed to be in the presence of God with their genitals exposed (Exod. 20:26; 28:42).[36] In other words, just as Adam was not allowed to appear naked in God's presence in the garden-temple, so subsequent priests had to be clothed while serving in the tabernacle or temple. Wenham notes that 'once again vocabulary associated with worship in the sanctuary is being used in Genesis'.[37]

Conclusion

Taking all of the evidence into account, there are well-founded exegetical reasons to conclude that the garden's primary purpose was not agricultural. While no single element is incontrovertible evidence that the garden was the first earthly temple, considering its features (location in the east on a mountain, river, trees, precious stones and metal, cherubim, God's presence and creation of the garden, man's responsibilities and his post-fall vestments), there is significant evidence that confirms the garden's temple status.

For these reasons Kline is certainly warranted when he writes that

> God produced in Eden a microcosmic version of his cosmic sanctuary. The garden planted there was holy ground with guardianship of its sanctity committed in turn to men and to cherubim. It was the temple-garden of God, the place chosen by the Glory-Spirit who hovered over creation from the beginning to be the focal site of his throne-presence among men. ... By virtue of this theophanic cloud-canopy, Eden had the character of a holy tabernacle, a microcosmic house of God. And since it was God himself who, present in his theophanic Glory,

---

[36]Gordon J. Wenham, *Genesis 1-15*, WBC, vol. 1 (Dallas: Word, 1987), p. 84; von Rad, *Genesis*, p. 91.

[37]Wenham, 'Sanctuary Symbolism,' pp. 401-02.

constituted the Edenic temple, man in the Garden of God could quite literally confess that Yahweh was his refuge and the Most High was his habitation.[38]

Kline's observations, however, are neither new nor unique, though perhaps ignored over the years. In the same way that the doctrine of the covenant was largely dormant in theological writing until the Reformation, so too the idea of the garden as a temple has been dormant.

Perhaps one of the earliest writings that identify the garden of Eden as a temple comes from the Jewish book of Jubilees (c. 75–50 BC): 'And he [Noah] knew that the garden of Eden was the holy of holies and the dwelling of the LORD. And Mount Sinai was in the midst of the desert and Mount Zion was in the midst of the navel of the earth. The three of these were created as holy places, one facing the other' (Jub. 8.19-20).[39] Though somewhat fragmentary in his formulation, Luther long ago wrote that God built Adam 'a temple that he may worship Him'.[40] In the 1950s Karl Barth made similar observations that appear to have gone unnoticed: 'The general nature of Paradise is that of a sanctuary.' Barth goes on to write that Adam

is specially brought there and given rest – an indication that the establishment of Paradise is a distinctive spatial parallel to the institution of the Sabbath as a temporal sanctuary in the first saga. The duty of man in this place is to cultivate and keep it – literally, to serve and watch over it – and it is no fancy if we see here the functions of the priests and Levites in the temple united in the person of one man. And as the tabernacle and later the temple had their center – not their geometrical but their

---

[38]Kline, *Images of the Spirit*, pp. 35-37; see also Poythress, *Shadow of Christ*, p. 31; Beale, *Temple*, 66.

[39]Beale, *Temple*, p. 78.

[40]Luther, *Genesis*, p. 95.

virtual and functional center – in the Holiest of Holies, so Eden had its center in the two trees specially planted by God alongside all the other trees, namely, the tree of life and the tree of the knowledge of good and evil.[41]

These conclusions about the setting of man in the creation have important implications for a proper understanding of the first three chapters of Genesis. Far from the generic presentation of man as a farmer who was commissioned by God to work in tending his vegetable garden and walk and talk with God when he came for visits, the presence of the temple set the activity of man in an entirely different light. Adam dwelt in the temple of God, like Samuel, who as a boy was taken to the temple 'that he may appear in the presence of the LORD and dwell there forever' (1 Sam. 1:22) and minister to him (1 Sam. 3:1). Adam was an archetypal priest, not a farmer. Scanning the horizon of redemptive history, we find further confirmation of the garden-temple thesis. At the end of redemptive history it is not a massive city-farm that descends out of the heavens, but a city-temple. If the end of redemptive history represents God's intentions from the beginning, then he planted a temple in Eden, not a farm. The next logical question is, What was the relational context in which Adam ministered to the Lord? Was Adam in a covenantal relationship?

---

[41]Barth, *Dogmatics*, vol. 3.1, pp. 253-54.

3

THE COVENANT OF WORKS

Introduction

The last chapter explored the characteristics of the garden and determined that it was not merely a center for agriculture but a primeval temple. One must now deal with the question of what type of relationship did God have with Adam. In other words, Was Adam in a covenantal relationship with God? The answer to this question is, Yes. Adam was in a covenantal relationship with God, a relationship historically called the *covenant of works*. The Westminster Confession states: 'The first covenant made with man was a covenant of works, wherein life was promised to Adam, and in him to his posterity, upon condition of perfect and personal obedience' (7.2). Though most within Reformed circles accept the doctrine of the covenant of works, there are many both within and without the Reformed camp who have called this doctrine into question, while others reject it outright.

This chapter will demonstrate that Adam was in a covenantal relationship with God and that this relationship is properly called a covenant of works. The chapter will therefore proceed along the following lines: (1) define what constitutes a covenant and give examples of Old Testament covenants; (2) examine the evidence found within Genesis 1–3 and the rest of Scripture to demonstrate the existence of a covenant in the garden; (3) determine what work Adam was required to perform in this covenant; (4) answer objections to these conclusions; and (5) draw some important connections concerning Adam's covenant with God and other key doctrinal loci.

Covenant defined

Definition
In the Old Testament, the Hebrew term used to denote a covenant is בְּרִית (bərît). What exactly is a בְּרִית (bərît)? A generic definition of a בְּרִית (bərît) is a treaty, alliance, or agreement between men or man and God, and it is typically translated in the Old Testament by the term *covenant*.[1] Taking into consideration the ancient Near Eastern cultural background, and more specifically the Hittite vassal-treaty (second millennium BC), there are some similarities between the covenants of the ancient Near East and the covenant in the book of Deuteronomy. There are typically six elements in Hittite-vassal treaties:

(1) titular introductions of the treaty participants, such as the title of the suzerain, or covenant lord, and his vassal, or servant;
(2) a historical prologue rehearsing past relationships;
(3) stipulations to the treaty;
(4) a clause requiring the treaty's regular reading and its preservation in a temple;
(5) blessings and curses for either keeping or breaking the treaty;
(6) a list of those who witness the treaty.

This is not to say that there is identical consonance between the treaties of the ancient Near East and the Bible, Deuteronomy in particular.[2] But one can see some of these characteristics in a small excerpt from the Hittite

---

[1]BDB, qv. בְּרִית, p. 136.
[2]Gordon J. McConville, 'בְּרִית' in NIDOTTE, vol. 1, p. 747.

treaty, Suppiluliumas and Aziras of Amurru: 'These are the words of the Sun Suppiluliumas, the great king, the king of the Hatti land, the valiant, the favorite of the Storm-god. I, the Sun, made you my vassal. And if you, Aziras, "protect" the king of the Hatti land, your master, the king of the Hatti land, your master, will "protect" you in the same way.'[3] While much of the content of the biblical covenants is unique, there is nevertheless enough similarity between the ancient Near East and the Old Testament covenants that 'the analogy of the treaties helps make the general point that Yahweh is Israel's suzerain and that the covenantal relationship demands for its preservation a certain commitment from the people.'[4] What about the covenants of the Old Testament?

Old Testament covenants
There are two major types of covenants that are found in the Old Testament: those between human parties and those between God and his people. In covenants between human parties there are several types:[5]

Friendship: such as David's covenant with Jonathan (1 Sam. 18:3; cf. 20:8).

Parity: between rulers or powerful individuals such as Abraham's covenant with Abimelech (Gen. 21:27; cf. 26:28; 31:44; 1 Kings 5:12; 15;19; 2 Kings 11:4).

Suzerain and vassal: a more powerful party sets the terms such as Joshua's treaty with the Gibeonites (Josh. 9:15; cf. 1 Sam. 11:1; Ezek. 17:13-18; Jer. 34:8).

Marriage: permanent union between a man and woman (Mal. 2:14; cf. Ezek. 16:8).

---

[3]ANE 2, p. 42.
[4]McConville, 'בְּרִית' p. 747.
[5]McConville, 'בְּרִית' p. 748.

The covenants between God and his people fall into the general category of suzerain and vassal. God is clearly, in any covenant, the more powerful party. Nevertheless, this does not mean that all of God's covenants with his people take on the exact same form. Some covenants are clearly unilateral, wholly depending upon God to execute and carry them out. Other covenants are bilateral in nature, and require a response on the part of God's people.[6] Within the Bible one finds several important major covenants:

Noahic: the covenant between God and Noah, but more broadly between God and the creation (Gen. 9:8-17). This covenant falls in the unilateral category, as it essentially consists of God's promise. God also has an accompanying sign of the covenant, the rainbow (Gen. 9:13).

Abrahamic: the covenant between God and Abraham (Gen. 15:18; 17:2), which also includes Abraham's posterity, land, and a continuing relationship with God, with the ultimate goal of the blessing of the nations. Though emphasis lies upon the unilateral administration of this covenant, the bilateral element is present in the expected response (Gen. 17:1, 9-14). This covenant also has a sign, circumcision (Gen. 17:9-14).

---

[6]McConville, 'בְּרִית' pp. 748-50. This is not to deny the sovereignty of God in his redemptive activities towards man. The bilateral aspects of a covenant do not admit synergism but recognize the importance of human responsibility. For a historical and theological treatment of these aspects of a covenant see Richard A. Muller, *Dictionary of Latin and Greek Theological Terms: Drawn Principally from Scholastic Theology* (Grand Rapids: Baker Books, 1985), pp. 120, 122, q.v. *foedus monopleuron* and *foedus dipleuron*; Lyle D. Bierma, 'Federal Theology in the Sixteenth Century: Two Traditions?' *WTJ* 45 (1983), pp. 304-21; cf. J. Wayne Baker, *Heinrich Bullinger and the Covenant: The Other Reformed Tradition* (Athens: Ohio University Press, 1980). There is also a balance between the uni- and bilateral elements in salvation in such confessional documents as the Westminster Confession of Faith (cf. §§ 3, 9).

Mosaic: the covenant between God and Israel on the occasion of their deliverance from Egypt (Exod. 19–24). Once again, while there are clearly unilateral elements in this covenant, that only God could deliver Israel, there is a greater emphasis upon the bilateral elements, keeping the covenant (19:5). This covenant is accompanied by the Decalogue (20:2-27) and the book of the covenant (21–23), which constitutes the covenant stipulations, a covenant ratification (24:3-8), a covenant meal (24:9-11), the construction of the tabernacle (Exod. 25–27), the consecration of the Aaronic priesthood (Exod. 28–29), and the ritual regulations of Leviticus. The most developed form of the Mosaic covenant appears in Deuteronomy, which bears strong resemblances to Hittite treaties.[7] This covenant builds upon the Abrahamic covenant, in that circumcision is still required by its male participants, but God gives the Israelites an additional sign of the covenant, the Sabbath (Exod. 31:13).

Davidic: the covenant between God and King David (2 Sam. 7:8-17). This covenant is a unilateral covenant because it contains no explicit conditions and is exclusively based upon the promise of God. It is described as a 'covenant of salt' (2 Chron. 13:5), which conveys the idea of permanence (cf. Lev. 2:13; esp. Num. 18:19). This covenant is rooted in the Mosaic and Abrahamic covenants.

While the description of the above listed covenants is not exhaustive, it nonetheless gives a framework out of which one may examine Genesis 1–3 and demonstrate that Adam was in a covenantal context.[8]

---

[7]Meredith G. Kline, *The Structure of Biblical Authority* (Eugene: Wipf & Stock, 1989), p. 37.

[8]For a more in-depth treatment of Old Testament covenants, see O. Palmer Robertson, *The Christ of the Covenants* (Phillipsburg: P & R, 1980).

Covenant in Genesis 1–3

Genesis 1–3

In Genesis 1–3 there are places within the narrative that give evidence of the covenantal context in which Adam serves and knows God. One must, therefore, begin with a survey of those elements. Then one must explore other important biblical passages to substantiate the claim that Adam was in a covenantal relationship with God. So, then, what about the creation narrative is covenantal?

When examining the initial creative acts of God, at first glance there does not appear to be evidence of any covenantal activity. For example, the author seems to report plainly the creation of day and night: 'God called the light Day, and the darkness he called Night' (Gen. 1:5). God merely gives day and night their names. Yet, it may surprise some readers to be informed that this is covenantal activity, even although Genesis 1 does not identify it as such.

Considering the creation of day and night from the prophet Jeremiah the investigator gains a great deal of relevant information. Jeremiah states:

> If you can break my covenant with the day and my covenant with the night, so that day and night will not come at their appointed time, then also my covenant with David my servant may be broken, so that he shall not have a son to reign on his throne, and my covenant with the Levitical priests my ministers (Jer. 33:20-21).

Nowhere in Genesis 1 does the reader have an indication that God has established a covenant with the day and night, yet Jeremiah clearly states this is the case. When God creates, it is covenantal. This is not the only way in which the covenantal aspect of God's creative activity surfaces in the opening verses of Genesis.

Comparing the creative imagery of Genesis 1, particularly of the Spirit of God hovering over the chaotic waters (v. 2), this same imagery reappears in other contexts that are clearly covenantal. In this regard, Meredith Kline writes:

> Special interest attaches to the appearance of the Glory-Spirit in a witness role in historical episodes or visionary scenes of re-creation that are repetitive of the original creation as described in Genesis 1.2. For besides confirming our identification of the Glory-Presence in Genesis 1.2, such evidence of the presence of God as a divine witness in Genesis 1.2 is an index of the covenantal cast of the whole creation narrative. Here we can simply suggest some of the data. In the exodus re-creation, the Glory-cloud, described by Moses by means of the imagery of Genesis 1.2, as we have seen, stood as pillar witness to the covenant that defined the legal nature of this redemptive action of God. At the beginning of the new creation, at the baptism of Jesus, the Spirit descending over the waters in avian form, as in Genesis 1.2, was a divine testimony to the Son, the Son who was given as God's covenant to the people. At the consummation of the new covenant with its new exodus-creation, the Glory-figure, apocalyptically revealed in Revelation 10.1ff, is seen clothed with a cloud, rainbow haloed, with the face like the sun and feet like pillars of fire, standing astride creation with his hand raised in oath to heaven, swearing by him who on the seventh day finished his creating of the heaven, the earth, the sea, and all their hosts that in the days of the seventh trumpet the mystery of God will be finished. In the interpretive light of such redemptive reproductions of the Genesis 1.2 scene, we see that the Spirit at the beginning overarched creation as a divine witness to the Covenant of Creation, as a sign that creation existed under the aegis of his covenant lordship.[9]

---

[9]Meredith G. Kline, *Images of the Spirit* (Eugene: Wipf & Stock, 1998), p. 19.

In these other covenantal contexts, the Holy Spirit is present as a witness to God's covenantal activity: the exodus, baptism of Christ, and the consummation. It stands to reason, then, that Kline's contention is correct – the Holy Spirit functioned in the same way at the beginning of the creation in Genesis 1:2. He was a witness to God's covenantal lordship. Gordon Spykman notes that 'the covenant is rooted in God's work of creation. God covenanted his world into existence. Covenantal relationships are given in, with, and for all created reality. From the beginning creation is unthinkable apart from its covenantal relationship of dependence and responsiveness *coram Deo*.'[10] It is clear, then, God's creative activity is covenantal.

There is more evidence that one should consider from Genesis 2–3. In these two chapters, there are several elements that demonstrate Adam's covenant relationship with God.

First, when God created Adam and placed him in the garden, the primeval temple, he issued a command that contains both blessing and curse (2:16-17). This parallels the commands given in the Mosaic covenant not only in verbal form but also with the appended blessings and curses (Exod. 20:2-27; cf. Gen. 2:16-17):[11]

Genesis 2:17	Hebrew	Exodus 20:13-15	Hebrew
You shall not eat	לֹא תֹאכַל (lōʾ tōʾkal)	You shall not murder	לֹא תִּרְצָח (lōʾ tirṣāh)
		You shall not commit adultery	לֹא תִנְאָף (lōʾ tinʾāp)
		You shall not steal	לֹא תִגְנֹב (lōʾ tignōb)

---

[10]Gordon J. Spykman, *Reformational Theology: A New Paradigm for Doing Dogmatics* (Grand Rapids: Eerdmans, 1992), p. 260.

[11]Claus Westermann, *Genesis 1-11*, trans. John J. Scullion

A second feature seen in Genesis 1–3 is the use of the trees of life and knowledge. What are and how do these respective trees function within the narrative? They closely parallel the signs of the Abrahamic, Noahic, and Mosaic covenants, circumcision (Gen. 17:9-14); the rainbow (Gen. 9:13-16); and the Sabbath (Exod. 31:13). A sign of the covenant typically functions as a visual reminder of the covenant between God and his servant. The two trees have a sacramental function similar to those sacramental signs of God's redemptive covenants, visible signs of God's invisible redemptive grace. While the two trees are not signs of grace, as Adam has yet to sin, they do function sacramentally by serving as visual reminders of God's stated blessing and curse, the promise of life or death. Seeing the trees of life and knowledge as sacramental is not a new observation; it is one found, for example, in John Calvin:

> The term 'sacrament' ... embraces generally all those signs which God has ever enjoined upon men to render them more certain and confident of the truth of his promises. He sometimes willed to present these in natural things, at other times set them forth in miracles. Here are some examples of the first kind. One is when he gave Adam and Eve the tree of life as a guarantee of immortality, that they might assure themselves of it as long as they should eat of its fruit. Another, when he set the rainbow for Noah and his descendants, as a token that he would not destroy the earth with a flood. These, Adam and Noah regarded as sacraments. Not that the tree provided them with an immortality which it could not give to itself; nor that the rainbow (which is but a reflection of the sun's rays upon the clouds opposite) could be effective in holding back the waters; but because they had a mark engraved upon them by

---

(Minneapolis: Fortress, 1994), p. 223; Nahum Sarna, *Genesis*, JPSTC (Philadelphia, JPS, 1989), p. 21; Martin Luther, *Lectures on Genesis*, LW, vol. 1, ed. Jaroslav Pelikan (St. Louis: Concordia, 1958), pp. 107-08.

God's Word, so that they were proofs and seals of his covenants.[12]

While the evidence of God's command and the sacramental function of the trees is possible proof of a covenant, when one fans out into the rest of Scripture he finds further corroboration that Adam and Eve were indeed in covenant with God. Spykman comments regarding these elements:

> Though the word 'covenant' (*berith*) does not appear in the creation account (Genesis 1, 2), the basic elements of classic covenant making are clearly present. They are evident in (a) the preamble with its prologue, introducing the Sovereign in his relationship to the second party, (b) the promises and obligations which define the community established by the covenantal pact, and (c) the blessing-and-curse formula, with its stated condition for fidelity and its stated penalty for infidelity.[13]

In other words, besides what has already been brought forth in the second and third items (b and c), Spykman identifies yet another element of which one should take notice, item (a), the preamble. The Israelite in covenant with God at Sinai, the time during which Genesis was compiled and written, would hear the familiar echo of Genesis 1 in Exodus 20:2. Moreover, he would take note of items (b) and (c), the promises and obligations and blessing and curse formula, as well as the sacramental trees and see the parallels with his own covenantal context. It seems far more likely that he would draw the conclusion that Adam was in covenant with God rather than not. One finds confirmation of this conclusion from early Jewish thought.

---

[12]John Calvin, *Institutes of the Christian Religion*, ed. John T. McNeill, trans. Ford Lewis Battles (Philadelphia: Westminster, 1960), 4.14.18, p. 1294.

[13]Spykman, *Reformational Theology*, p. 260.

For example, in the *Testament of Moses*, one reads of what supposedly happened after the fall: 'And the Lord, coming into paradise, set his throne, and called with a dreadful voice, saying, Adam, where are you and why are you hidden from my face? Shall the house be hidden from him that built it? And he says, Since you have forsaken my covenant, I have brought upon your body seventy strokes.'[14]

There is also a parallel in the Old Testament apocrypha: 'The Lord created human beings out of earth. ... He bestowed knowledge upon them, and allotted to them the law of life. He established with them an eternal covenant, and revealed to them his decrees' (Sir. 17:1, 11-12).

One sees, then, that the idea that Adam was in covenant with God has ancient pedigree, long before the church father Augustine or the sixteenth-century Reformers brought forth their explanations.

There are further considerations from God's covenantal dealings with Noah that bear upon the idea of a covenant between Adam and God.

Genesis 6:18

The term *covenant* is first used in God's dealings with Noah: 'But I will establish my covenant with you' (Gen. 6:18a). By way of contrast, when God initiates his covenant with Abraham one finds different nomenclature than what is found in 6:18. Instead of the term הקם (hăqīm), or 'establish', one finds the term כרת (kārat), 'the LORD *made* a covenant with Abram' (Gen. 15:18, emphasis mine). Literally translated, the term כרת (kārat) means 'to cut', hence God 'cut' a covenant with Abraham. The term כרת (kārat) reappears at the initiation of subsequent covenants such as between Abraham and Abimelech (Gen. 21:27, 32; cf. 26:28; 31:44), God and Israel at Sinai (Exod. 34:10), and in the prohibition

---

[14]*ANF*, vol. 8, p. 565.

to initiate a covenant with the Gentile inhabitants of the promised land (Exod. 23:32; cf. Gen. 17:2). What is the significance of the different nomenclature in Genesis 6:18 and 15:18?

Genesis 6:18 does not refer to the initiation of a new covenant but rather the continuation of an already existing covenant. The use of the verb הקם (hăqīm) suggests the reestablishment of something already in place.[15] In fact, William Dumbrell argues that Genesis 6:18 'refers to a divine relationship established by the fact of creation itself.' For this reason, there is the 'absence of standard terminology of covenant initiation from the early Genesis narratives'.[16] This has important implications for God's subsequent covenantal dealings with Noah in Genesis 9. When God makes his covenant with Noah in Genesis 9, there are clear connections between verses 1-2 and the dominion mandate of Genesis 1:28. The Noahic covenant is rooted in creation and, as Dumbrell notes, 'any theology of covenant must begin with Genesis 1:1.'[17] If this analysis of Genesis 6:18 is correct, then it means that God established a covenant with Adam and that the covenant concept does not arise *de novo* in God's dealings with Noah.

There is another important Old Testament reference that confirms that man was in covenant with God in the garden.

Hosea 6:7

Within the history of Bible interpretation there are some verses that have received much attention with little to no consensus achieved by those who interpret them. Hosea 6:7 is just such a verse: וְהֵמָּה כְּאָדָם עָבְרוּ בְרִית (wǝhēmmāh kǝ'āḏām 'āḇrû ḇǝrît): 'But like men [or Adam]

---

[15]McConville, 'בְּרִית' p. 748.

[16]W. J. Dumbrell, *Covenant and Creation: A Theology of the Old Testament Covenants* (1984; Carlisle: Paternoster, 1984), p. 32, see esp. pp. 25ff.

[17]Dumbrell, *Covenant and Creation*, p. 42.

they transgressed the covenant.' There is disagreement over exactly how the phrase כְּאָדָם (kə'āḏām) should be translated. There are those who believe it should be rendered as 'like man' (LXX; NKJV; KJV). On the other hand, there are those who believe it should be translated as 'like Adam' (Vul.; NRSV; NASV; ESV; NIV). The implications of a correct translation are significant. If the correct translation of the verse is 'like Adam', then there is a clear and explicit affirmation of the existence of a covenant between Adam and God. Which of the two possible translations is preferable?[18]

There are those who argue that Hosea 6:7 should be translated as 'But like men they transgressed the covenant'. Calvin argues that Hosea states that the Israelites have 'showed themselves to be men in violating the covenant'.[19] For Calvin, the intended comparison is between the faithfulness of God and the faithlessness of the sinful Israelites – they have acted like sinful men. Regarding the possibility of the alternative translation of 'like Adam', Calvin rather brusquely comments: 'I do not stop to refute this comment; for we see that it is in itself vapid.'[20]

Yet, as B. B. Warfield notes, if the comparison is to men in general, it lacks the needed specificity with the bare use of the term *men*. Warfield writes that 'the simple "men" must be made in some way to bear a pregnant sense – either as mere men, as opposed to God, or as

---

[18]These are not the only two options. There are those who hold that it should be translated as, 'they have treated my covenant as if it was dirt' (Douglas Stuart, *Hosea-Jonah*, WBC, vol. 31 [Dallas: Word Books, 1987], p. 111). There are others who believe that this is a reference to the city of Adam (Josh. 3:16) (Francis I. Anderson and David Noel Freedman, *Hosea*, AB, vol. 24 [New York: Double Day, 1980], p. 439). Cf. Thomas McComiskey, *Hosea*, The Minor Prophets, vol. 1, ed. Thomas McComiskey (Grand Rapids: Baker, 1992), p. 95.

[19]John Calvin, *Hosea*, CTS, vol. 13 (rep.; Grand Rapids: Baker, 1993), p. 235.

[20]Calvin, *Hosea*, p. 235.

common men as opposed to the noble or the priestly, or as heathen as opposed to the Israelites – to none of which does it seem naturally to lend itself here – before a significance equal to the demands of its context is given it.[21] The most natural reading of the verse is a comparison between Adam, God's son (Luke 3:38), and Israel who is also God's son (Exod. 4:22-23).

Warfield draws upon the parallels between Adam and Israel when he favorably quotes another author who writes that

> God in his great goodness had planted Adam in Paradise, but Adam violated the commandment which prohibited his eating of the tree of knowledge, and thereby transgressed the covenant of his God. Loss of fellowship with God and expulsion from Eden were the penal consequences that immediately followed. Israel like Adam had been settled by God in Palestine, the glory of all lands; but ungrateful for God's great bounty and gracious gift, they broke the covenant of their God, the condition of which, as in the case of the Adamic covenant, was obedience.[22]

Based upon Warfield's evidence, it seems that 'like Adam' is the more natural and powerful comparison and that Hosea 6:7 may be cited in support of the idea that Adam was in a covenantal relationship with God.[23] One finds corroborating evidence with the similar use of כְּאָדָם (kəʾāḏām) in Job 31:33: 'If I have covered my transgressions as Adam' (NKJV; NASV; ASV; KJV). Warfield acknowledges that he is not the only one to come to this conclusion and that other luminaries such as Martin Luther, Francis Turretin, Wilhelmus à Brakel, Herman

---

[21]B. B. Warfield, 'Hosea 6.7: Adam or Man?,' in *Collected Shorter Writings*, ed. John E. Meeter, vol. 1 (1970; Phillipsburg: Presbyterian & Reformed, 2001), p. 127.

[22]Warfield, 'Hosea 6.7,' pp. 128-29.

[23]So McComiskey, *Hosea*, p. 95. This is the view of rabbinic interpreters (see *Mid. Rabb.* Lam.Pro. 4).

Witsius, Franz Delitzsch, A. A. Hodge, Herman Bavinck and Geerhardus Vos hold the same view.[24] One may also add that the American revisions of the Westminster Confession of Faith (1789) cite this passage in support of the covenant of works. While this is not proof that this interpretation is correct, one may affirm with Warfield that 'if we should err, we should err in a great and goodly company'.[25]

Moving forward, then, one may proceed to examine a key New Testament passage that demonstrates that Adam was in a covenantal relationship with God in the garden.

Romans 5:12-19
In these verses the apostle Paul sets up a clear parallel between the first and second Adam, namely Jesus Christ (cf. 1 Cor. 15:45). There is no doubt regarding Christ as the mediator of the new covenant (Matt. 26:28; Heb. 9:15; 12:24). There is a key connection between Adam and Christ when Paul identifies Adam as a τύπος (tupos) or 'a type of the one who was to come' (Rom. 5:14). N. T. Wright states that Paul does not use τύπος in a general

---

[24]Francis Turretin, *Institutes of Elenctic Theology*, 3 vols., ed. James T. Dennison, trans. George Musgrave Giger (Phillipsburg: P & R, 1992-97), vol. 1, 8.3.8, p. 576; Wilhelmus à Brakel, *The Christian's Reasonable Service*, 4 vols., trans. Bartel Elshout (Morgan: Soli Deo Gloria, 1992), vol. 1, p. 363-65; Herman Witsius, *Economy of the Covenants Between God and Man*, trans. William Crookshank (1822; Phillipsburg: P & R, 1990), vol. 1, 2.15–3.8, pp. 58-64; C. F. Keil and Frans Delitzsch, *Commentary on the Old Testament*, 10 vols. (1866-91; Peabody: Hendrickson, 1996), vol. 10, p. 66; A. A. Hodge, *Outlines of Theology* (1860; Edinburgh: Banner of Truth, 1991), p. 310; Herman Bavinck, *In the Beginning: Foundations of Creation Theology*, trans. John Vriend, ed. John Bolt (Grand Rapids: Baker Books, 1999), p. 199; Geerhardus Vos, *Biblical Theology: Old and New Testaments* (1948; Edinburgh: Banner of Truth, 1996), p. 34. For a historical survey of the interpretation of Hosea 6:7 within the Reformed tradition see Richard A. Muller, *Post-Reformation Reformed Dogmatics*, vol. 2, *Holy Scripture: The Cognitive Foundation of Theology* (Grand Rapids: Baker Books, 1993), pp. 456-63.

[25]Warfield, 'Adam or Man?,' p. 129.

but in a technical sense. The thought is that Paul uses τύπος to convey the idea of a die or stamp that leaves an impression on wax. In other words, 'Adam prefigured the Messiah in certain respects.'[26] C. E. B. Cranfield notes more specifically that when τύπος is used in its technical sense it is a 'person or thing prefiguring (according to God's design) a person or thing pertaining to the time of eschatological fulfillment. Adam, in his universal effectiveness for ruin, is the type which – in God's design – prefigures Christ in His universal effectiveness for salvation.'[27] It is important to realize that Paul's comparison between Adam and Christ, therefore, is not coincidental or convenient but predetermined by God himself.[28]

Is one to conclude that Christ as the antitype merited the salvation within a covenantal context but that Adam, the type, was not in such a context? It is not impossible to assume this conclusion but it certainly runs against the grain of Scripture if one eliminates a covenantal context for Adam. Luther, approvingly quoting Augustine, writes that 'just as Adam has become a cause of death to those who are born of him, even though they have not eaten of the tree, the death brought on by the eating, so also Christ was made a provider of righteousness for those who belong to Him, even though they are entirely lacking in righteousness.'[29] Now, in what context does Augustine elsewhere place Adam?

Augustine places Adam in the context of a covenant. Augustine writes in his *City of God* concerning

---

[26]N. T. Wright, *Romans*, NIB, vol. 10 (Nashville: Abingdon, 2003), p. 527.

[27]C. E. B. Cranfield, *Romans*, vol. 1, ICC (1975; Edinburgh: T & T Clark, 2001), p. 283; see also Leonhard Goppelt, *Typos: The Typological Interpretation of the Old Testament in the New*, trans. Donald H. Madvig (1939; Grand Rapids: Eerdmans, 1982), pp. 129-30.

[28]For other views see James D. G. Dunn, *Romans 1-8*, WBC, vol. 38a (Dallas: Word Books, 1988), pp. 277-79.

[29]Augustine, *Contra Julianum* 1.6.22, as cited in Martin Luther,

Romans 5:12 that 'even the infants, not personally in their own life, but according to the common origin of the human race, have all broken God's covenant in that one in whom all have sinned.' Augustine is not unaware, however, that neither Romans 5:12, nor Genesis 1–3 explicitly states that Adam was in the context of a covenant. He goes on to write that 'there are many things called God's covenants besides those two great ones, the old and the new, which any one who pleases may read and know. For the first covenant, which was made with the first man, is just this: "In the day you eat thereof, you shall surely die." '[30]

Based upon the parallel between Christ and Adam, the technical use of τύπος, the covenantal context in which Christ as the second Adam brings redemption, one may conclude that Adam was also in a covenantal context. In fact, Douglas Moo comments that the 'similarity between Adam's relationship to his "descendants" and Christ's to his underlies all of vv. 15-21.'[31] Romans 5:12-21 not only tells of the existence of a covenant between God and Adam in protology, it helps the reader understand the pattern in eschatology with the work of the second Adam. Charles Hodge notes that as

Adam was the head and representative of his race, whose destiny was suspended on his conduct, so Christ is the head and representative of his people. As the sin of the one was the ground of our condemnation, so the righteousness of the other is the ground of our justification. This relation between Adam and the Messiah was recognized by the Jews, who called their expected deliverer, אָדָם הָאַחֲרוֹן, *the last Adam*, as Paul also

---

Lectures on Romans, LW, vol. 25, trans. Jacob A. O. Preus (Saint Louis: Concordia, 1972), p. 305.

[30]Augustine, *City of God*, trans. Marcus Dodds, NPNF, 16.29, p. 326b.

[31]Douglas Moo, *Epistle to the Romans*, NICNT (Grand Rapids: Eerdmans, 1996), p. 334.

calls him in 1 Cor. 15:45, ὁ ἔσχατος Ἀδάμ, Adam was the type, τοῦ μέλλοντος, either of the *Adam* who was to come, or simply *of the one to come.* The Old Testament system was preparatory and prophetic. The people under its influence were looking forward to the accomplishment of the promises made to their father. The Messianic period on which their hopes were fixed was called 'the world or age to come,' and the Messiah himself was ὁ ἐρχόμενος, ὁ μέλλων, *the one coming.*[32]

In addition to establishing Adam's covenantal relationship with God, the connection with Christ as the second Adam also begins to demonstrate other key links between protology, christology, soteriology, and eschatology. As James Dunn notes, 'Christ is the eschatological counterpart of primeval Adam.'[33] Several conclusions concerning the covenant of works are in order at this point before the investigation proceeds.

Conclusions

Various examples and types of covenants within Scripture have been given. Narrowing the scope of the investigation to the question of whether Adam was in a covenantal relationship with God, the chapter has surveyed several key elements within Genesis 1–3 and the greater scope of Scripture. Key elements that the investigation has identified are that when God created, he did not create apart from a theological context. Indeed, God created the world and administers his kingdom covenantally. Though Genesis 1 does not report the covenant nature of God's creative activity, Jeremiah 33:20ff certainly sheds light upon the fact that he created in terms of a covenant. The prologue of Genesis 1, God's command to Adam, the blessing and curse attached to it, and the sacramental trees of

---

[32]Charles Hodge, *Romans* (1835; Edinburgh: Banner of Truth, 1989), p. 162.
[33]Dunn, *Romans*, p. 277.

life and knowledge, are further indicators that Adam was in covenant with God. These elements parallel those found in subsequent covenants in Scripture. The chapter then examined Genesis 6:18, Hosea 6:7, and Romans 5:12-19 (esp. v. 14) to demonstrate that God confirmed an already existing covenant with Noah, and that that covenant was one that he had made with Adam. Any one of these factors by themselves would not constitute irrefutable evidence, but all of them together lead to the conclusion that Adam was in a covenantal context with God.

One should also note that while the term *covenant* does not occur in Genesis 1–3, the rest of Scripture confirms its existence. The implied existence of the covenant is much like the implied existence of the covenantal relationship between Adam and Eve. The author, for example, refers to the woman as Adam's 'wife' (Gen. 2:24), and he refers to the man as the woman's 'husband' (Gen. 3:6). There is no mention of a marriage ceremony, though the reader may nonetheless say that Adam and Eve were in a covenantal relationship, one that Scripture characterizes as the marriage bond (Mal. 2:14). The question to which one must now turn is, What was the nature of the covenant? What was Adam required to do in his covenantal relationship with God?

The work of the covenant

The dominion mandate
Now that Adam's covenantal relationship with God has been established, one must determine what duties or responsibilities Adam was required to fulfill. Unlike unilateral covenants that God makes, such as those with the day and night or with the post-flood creation, God's other covenants are bilateral and require a response on the part of the one with whom God has covenanted. The clearest statement of man's covenant responsibilities is found in what many call the dominion mandate: 'Be

fruitful and multiply and fill the earth and subdue it and have dominion over the fish of the sea and over the birds of the heavens and over every living thing that moves on the earth' (Gen. 1:28).

Adam was given several tasks in this command from God: (1) fill the earth with the image of God through procreation; (2) subdue the earth; and (3) have dominion over the creation, that is, exercise authority over it. Not only was Adam supposed to carry out this work of expansion, but there was also an end to Adam's labors represented in the Sabbath rest.

Adam was given a period of probation in the garden, and had he passed the probation and eaten from the tree of life, he would have passed the days of his life carrying about his work of expansion until he completed the work.

At this point, one may give Adam's work the title of 'expansion', and so one must ask, Why was Adam given this expansion task? What precisely was Adam supposed to expand?

The dominion mandate misunderstood
One can find statements in both scholarly and popular literature regarding the nature of Adam's work in the garden. Concerning Genesis 2:15, for example, John Murray writes:

> Here is explicit allusion to Adam's specific employment, and we must recognize that such labor is not a curse but a blessing. It finds its ground and sanction in the fact that man's life is patterned after the divine exemplar established in the creation and formation of the universe which constitutes the realm of man's existence and activity. That Adam's labor consisted in dressing the garden and keeping it informs us that it was highly worthy of man's dignity as created after the divine image to be employed in so mundane a task.[34]

There are similar statements in popular literature as well; for example, R. C. Sproul writes:

> We were created to dress, till, and keep the earth. We were made to be fruitful – to be productive as God is productive. And God assigned us these tasks before the Fall. Thus, labor is not a curse; it is a blessing that goes with Creation. The sanctity of human labor is rooted in the work of God Himself and in His call to us to imitate Him.[35]

Commentators such as Murray and Sproul take work as a creation ordinance and then extrapolate that work in general is part of man's responsibilities. This line of thinking is aptly captured by Sproul when he writes:

> A person's labor is sacred. It cannot prosper if mismatched with corporate goals or missions. Blessed is the person whose personal mission is in harmony with the mission of the group. In this situation, both the individual and the group can work together for the glory of God, and escape alienation from labor.[36]

But is this how one should understand Adam's covenant responsibilities? Was Adam merely to work? Was he merely to keep the garden? Was Adam primarily a farmer? As previously argued, this is not the case; there was a specific goal to Adam's covenantal work.

The dominion mandate in its temple context
It is important to pay close attention to minute details in Genesis 1–3. There are several elements in these chapters that provide important information concerning the intended goal of Adam's covenantal work.

---

[34]John Murray, *Principles of Conduct: Aspects of Biblical Ethics* (1957; Grand Rapids: Eerdmans, 2001), p. 35.
[35]R.C. Sproul, 'Like Father, Like Son,' *Tabletalk*, July 2003, p. 7.
[36]Sproul, 'Like Father, Like Son,' p. 7.

First, the investigation has established that Adam was not merely a farmer but first and foremost a priest. As Gordon Wenham notes, 'Adam should be regarded as an archetypal Levite.'[37]

Second, the garden of Eden is not a farm but the first temple, the place in which Adam must perform his priestly labor.

Third, recall that Adam was created in the image of the triune Lord and was given vicegerency over the creation. Just as God rules over the cosmos, so too Adam must rule over the creation under God's authority (Gen. 1:26; Ps. 8).

Fourth, there was a difference between the conditions inside and outside the garden. Genesis 2:5 states that 'bush of the field was yet in the land', a reference to field vegetation fit only for animal grazing. On the other hand, 'no small plant of the field had yet sprung up,' a reference to agriculture grown with irrigation and human effort for consumption as food.[38]

This division between field vegetation and cultivated agriculture means that there was a noticeable boundary between the garden and the outside world. God sent rain and created man to grow food (Gen. 2:6-7),(pp. 97-98) and therefore in the immediate area of the garden there was order.[39]

---

[37]Gordon J. Wenham, 'Sanctuary Symbolism in the Garden of Eden Story,' in *I Studied Inscriptions from Before the Flood: Ancient Near Eastern, Literary, and Linguistic Approaches to Genesis 1–11*, eds Richard S. Hess and David Toshio Tsumura, Sources for Biblical and Theological Study, v. 4 (Winona Lake: Eisenbrauns, 1994), p. 401.

[38]See Gordon J. Wenham, *Genesis 1–15*, WBC, vol. 1 (Dallas: Word, 1987), p. 58; Derek Kidner, *Genesis*, TOTC (Downers Grove: InterVarsity, 1967), p. 59; Westermann, *Genesis*, p. 199; cf. Umberto Cassuto, *A Commentary on the Book of Genesis*, Part One, *From Adam to Noah*, trans. Israel Abrahams (Jerusalem: Magnes Press, 1998), pp. 101-02.

[39]See Meredith G. Kline, 'Because It Had Not Rained,' *WTJ* 20/2 (1958), pp. 146-57; and Mark D. Futato, 'Because It Had Rained,' *WTJ* 60/1 (1998), pp. 1-21.

These verses are typically understood to convey the idea that rain was not the normal means by which God caused things to grow. The NKJV says that a 'mist' watered the ground. The NIV, on the other hand, says that 'streams came up from the earth'. These are the two most popular interpretative options for this verse – either a mist or streams of water.[40]

The main point of the common interpretations is that prior to the flood it did not rain. But upon closer examination there appears to be a better translation and understanding of this verse. The challenge comes because the word that is translated here as 'mist', namely אֵד (ēḏ) is only found in one other place in the Bible: 'For he draws up drops of water, which distill as rain from the mist [אֵד / ēḏ], which the clouds drop down and pour abundantly on man' (Job 36:27-28). If these verses from Job give any interpretive direction for how one should understand the word אֵד (ēḏ), they rule out the translation offered by the NIV. The verse from Job distinctly says that God 'draws up' water, negating the idea that this is a reference to subterranean streams of water.

Additionally, these two verses from Job appear to be a synonymous parallelism. Thus the 'mist' is a synonym, albeit an uncommon one, for 'cloud'.[41] This is confirmed by ancient Jewish Targums, which render the word אֵד (ēḏ) in Aramaic as עֲנָן (ʿānān) or 'cloud'. Though the LXX renders אֵד (ēḏ) as πηγή (pêgê) or a 'spring' in Genesis 2:6, it translates the same term as νεφέλη (nephelê), or 'cloud', in Job 36:27.[42]

Some commentators argue that the water comes up from subterranean springs because the verse says that

---

[40]Calvin, p. 111; Luther, p. 83; Morris, pp. 84-85; Kidner, pp. 59-60. Some argue that this refers to subterranean springs: LXX; Wenham, pp. 58-59; Cassuto, pp. 103-04; Westermann, pp. 200-01; Gunkel, pp. 5-6.

[41]See Mitchell Dahood, 'Eblaite *i-du* and Hebrew *ʿd*, "Rain Cloud,"' *CBQ* 43/4 (1981), pp. 534-38.

[42]Contra Kenneth Gentry and Michael Butler, *Yea, Hath God Said?* (Eugene: Wipf & Stock, 2002), p. 114.

the mist 'came up [עלה / ʿlh] from the earth'.[43] If one compares 'a mist went up from the earth' with similar phrases in Scripture he discovers that the description is phenomenological, not literalistic: 'He it is who makes the clouds rise [עלה / ʿlh] at the end of the earth' (Ps. 135:7; RSV); and 'Behold, a little cloud like a man's hand is rising [עלה / ʿlh] out of the sea' (1 Kings 18.44). Clearly, this is a common way of describing rain clouds on the horizon. The clouds appear as though they are coming up from the earth.[44] There is a similar understanding of the relationship between rain, mist, and the horizon in the Qumran *Hymn to the Creator*: 'He made lightnings for the rain, and raised mist from the end [of the earth].'[45] Therefore, the preferable interpretation of verse 6 is that God sent rain clouds, not streams, to water the face of the ground.[46]

This is not a unique conclusion, as Keil similarly comments that 'the mist אד [ēd] vapor, which falls as rain, Job 36:27) is correctly regarded by Delitzsch as the creative beginning of the rain itself, from which we may infer, therefore, that it rained before the flood'.[47] The provision of rain, then, is the solution to the first of the stated problems, the absence of rain. Barth poignantly comments that 'did it not say previously that God had not yet sent rain upon the earth? What else, then, are we to expect but that He now caused it to rain?'[48] Vegetation throughout the globe and in the garden did not grow because they required water to grow. So, God sent a rain cloud to water the face of the earth.[49]

---

[43]Westermann, p. 201; Waltke, p. 84.

[44]Futato, 'Because It Rained,' pp. 6-8.

[45]DSS 2QPs^a = 2Q5, 4Q88, 26, ln. 15.

[46]Cf. Young, *Genesis*, pp. 62-63, n. 50.

[47]Keil, v. 1, p. 48.

[48]Karl Barth, *Church Dogmatics*, vol. 3.1, *The Doctrine of Creation*, trans. J. W. Edwards (1958; Edinburgh: T & T Clark, 1998), p. 241.

[49]See similar comments by Young, *Genesis*, p. 63. One should also note the understanding of rain in the Qumran community. Rain was not viewed as a result of the fall but as a source of blessing upon man (see DSS 2Q10, 4Q157, 19). This was also true of rabbinic opinions regarding rain (see *Mid. Rabb. Gen.* 6.4).

Outside the garden, however, there was less order, because man was not cultivating the ground. The bottom line is, inside the garden there was order maintained by Adam, whereas outside the garden there was disorder. This is not to say that God created chaos outside the garden but that in the same way that God brought order to the initial chaos of Genesis 1:1, so too Adam was to expand the garden-order throughout the world. These factors give an interpretive key and trajectory that help set Adam's covenantal work in the proper context.

Adam's covenantal work is not merely that of farming for six days and then resting on the seventh. Rather, God covenanted with Adam to: (1) multiply the image of God through procreation; (2) fill the earth with the image of God and expand the garden-temple to fill the earth – to bring the garden-order to the earth where there was no order – to subdue the earth; and (3) expand his vicegerency throughout the whole earth by having men, made in God's image, rule over the entire creation. Along these lines John Walton comments that

> if people were going to fill the earth, we must conclude that they were not intended to stay in the garden in a static situation. Yet moving out of the garden would appear a hardship since the land outside the garden was not as hospitable as that inside the garden (otherwise the garden would not be distinguishable). Perhaps, then, we should surmise that people were gradually supposed to extend the garden as they went about subduing and ruling. Extending the garden would extend the food supply as well as extend sacred space (since that is what the garden represented. In this regard it is possible to conclude that the inclusion of where the rivers went (2:11-14) is intended to indicate some of the resources that would eventually be at humankind's disposal as they worked their way out from the garden. Gold, spices, and precious stones all found their most common functions within sacred space, and these could be procured for that purpose as the garden was expanded.[50]

Walton, however, is not alone in this observation, as it was first made by Karl Barth some fifty years earlier:

> That the closed sanctuary with its trees has a symbolic or sacramental character is now revealed by the fact that the water which nourishes it does not take the form of a sea fed by a subterranean source and with subterranean exits, but that a whole river bursts forth which Eden is not to keep to itself but to take its own share and then to pass on to surrounding districts, and which is sufficiently powerful to divide into four parts – obviously indicating the four quarters of the compass – and to bring to these four quarters and therefore to the whole earth what it had brought to Eden.[51]

This sets Adam's covenantal work on an entirely different trajectory than one typically finds. Adam's mandate is not merely to labor but to expand the garden-temple throughout the earth, fill the earth with the image of God, and subdue it by spreading the glory of God to the ends of the earth. This is what constitutes Adam's covenant responsibilities. Adam, however, was not tasked with this work indefinitely. There was a terminus to his covenantal labors.

The goal of Adam's covenant of works: the Sabbath rest
God's own work of six days and a seventh day of rest indicates that Adam was to emulate this pattern in his own work. How long this work would have taken is unknown. How long Adam's probation would have lasted is also unknown. Little is known about Adam's

---

[50]John H. Walton, *Genesis*, NIVAC (Grand Rapids: Zondervan, 2001), pp. 186-87.

[51]Karl Barth, *Church Dogmatics*, vol. 3.1, *The Doctrine of Creation*, trans. J. W. Edwards (1958; Edinburgh: T & T Clark, 1998), p. 255. Similar ideas emerge from the Qumran community where they speak of the rivers of Eden that cause the boughs of an everlasting plant to grow and cover the whole earth (1QH14[10] 14 [6], ln. 17ff; also 1QH18[14]).

exact relationship to the tree of life. Had Adam refused the temptation of the serpent, that is, Satan (Rev. 12:9; 20:2), would he then have eaten from the tree of life and been enabled to carry out his work unhindered by the *posse peccare*, the power to sin, the possibility of abandoning his covenant with God? To this question, there is no firm answer. One may nevertheless recognize that Adam's state in the garden was never intended to be a permanent one. Adam had the responsibility of fulfilling his covenantal obligations, after which he would have entered into a permanent Sabbath rest. The probation would have ended, death would no longer have been a possibility, *posse non mori*, and Adam would have rested from his duties as vicegerent over the creation once the earth was filled with the image and glory of God.

In this regard Rowland Ward notes, 'We can say there was an eschatology before there was sin, that is, a glorious destiny was in view of which the tree of life in Genesis 2 was also a token. Creation at the beginning was not like it will be in the end, when it will be richer and more enduring.'[52] Stated more technically, Geerhardus Vos writes that 'the so-called "Covenant of Works" was nothing but an embodiment of the Sabbatical principle. Had its probation been successful, then the sacramental Sabbath would have passed over into the reality it typified, and the entire subsequent course of the history of the race would have been radically different.'[53] The conclusions, however, regarding Adam's labor and, more specifically, the covenant of works have not gone unchallenged.

Critics of the covenant of works

The affirmation of the covenant of works first existed in the earliest days of the church with Augustine's explanation of Genesis 2:16-17, but was somewhat

---

[52]Rowland S. Ward, *God & Adam: Reformed Theology and the Creation Covenant* (Wantirna: New Melbourne Press, 2003), p. 23.

[53]Vos, *Biblical Theology*, p. 140.

dormant throughout the Middle Ages. It was in the post-Reformation period that the doctrine of the covenant of works became normative in Reformed theology.[54] In the Westminster Confession of Faith (1646) the doctrine was codified (WCF 7.2). Despite the ascendancy and acceptance of the covenant of works in Reformed theology, the covenant of works has not been without its critics.[55] In recent years one of the most notable critics has been John Murray. Murray writes concerning the covenant of works:

> There are two observations. (1) The term is not felicitous, for the reason that the elements of grace entering into the administration are not properly provided for by the term 'works.' (2) It is not designated a covenant in Scripture. Hosea 6.7 may be interpreted otherwise and does not provide the basis for such a construction of the Adamic economy. Besides, Scripture always uses the term covenant, when applied to God's administration to men, in reference to a provision that is redemptive or closely related to redemptive design. Covenant in Scripture denotes the oath-bound confirmation of promise and involves a security which the Adamic economy did not bestow.[56]

One should examine Murray's argument point by point to demonstrate that he is incorrect in his rejection of the covenant of works. Within Murray's statement there are three major claims: (1) that because of the elements

---

[54]See J. V. Fesko, *Diversity within the Reformed Tradition: Supra- and Infralapsarianism in Calvin, Dort, and Westminster* (Greenville: Reformed Academic Press, 2003), pp. 222-35.

[55]For a good historical survey of the covenant of works, and the doctrine of the covenant in general, see Geerhardus Vos, 'The Doctrine of the Covenant in Reformed Theology,' in *Redemptive History and Biblical Interpretation: The Shorter Writings of Geerhardus Vos*, ed. Richard B. Gaffin (Phillipsburg: Presbyterian & Reformed, 1980), pp. 234-70.

[56]John Murray, *Collected Writings of John Murray*, vol. 2, *Systematic Theology* (1977; Banner of Truth, 1996), p. 49.

of grace present in Adam's probation in the garden, the term *works* is not a proper label; (2) that Scripture does not designate Adam's state in the garden under the term *covenant*; and (3) that Scripture always uses the term *covenant* in God's redemptive dealings with man.

The term 'works' is an inappropriate label

It is important first to acknowledge what characterizes Murray's conception of the term *covenant*. He writes that in order for one to comprehend the essence of a covenant, he must turn to God's post-diluvian dealings with Noah.[57] Murray explains that the Noahic covenant is 'intensely and pervasively monergistic. Nothing exhibits this more clearly than the fact that the sign attached to attest and seal the divine faithfulness and the irrevocability of God's promise is one produced by conditions over which God alone has control and in connection with which there is rigid exclusion of human co-operation.'[58]

One must recognize that Murray understands God's covenantal dealings with man in a unilateral fashion. In this connection Murray does not agree with the typical analysis and definitions of a covenant; he writes:

> It is quite apparent that in this covenant we must not take our point of departure from the idea of compact, or contract, or agreement in any respect whatsoever. It is not contractual in its origin, or in its constitution, or in its operation, or in its outcome. Its fulfillment or continuance is not in the least degree contingent even upon reciprocal obligation or appreciation on the part of its beneficiaries.[59]

Notice how Murray has defined a covenant. He has substantively defined a covenant as a sovereign admini-

---

[57]John Murray, *The Covenant of Grace: Biblical & Theological Studies* (London: Tyndale, 1954), p. 12.

[58]Murray, *Covenant*, pp. 12-13.

[59]Murray, *Covenant*, pp. 14-15.

stration of God's grace and promise; an administration that is unilateral in nature.[60] Given this definition, one has the reason why Murray rejects the term *works* in connection with Adam's pre-fall condition. He believes that God's dealings with Adam were not on the basis of justice but of grace. Along these lines he writes:

> In connection with the promise of life it does not appear justifiable to appeal, as frequently has been done, to the principle enunciated in certain texts (cf. Lev. 18:5; Rom. 10:5; Gal. 3:12, 'This do and thou shalt live.' The principle asserted in these texts is the principle of equity that righteousness is always followed by the corresponding award. From the promise of the Adamic administration we must dissociate all notions of meritorious reward. The promise of confirmed integrity and blessedness was one annexed to an obedience that Adam owed and, therefore, was a promise of grace. All that Adam could have claimed on the basis of equity was justification and life as long has he perfectly obeyed, but not confirmation so as to insure indefectibility. Adam could claim the fulfillment of the promise if he stood the probation, but only on the basis of God's faithfulness, not on the basis of justice.[61]

The belief that Adam stood by God's grace in his relationship with God is key to Murray's conception of man's state in the garden. Because Adam stood by grace, he could not pass the probation on the basis of justice.

Considering Murray's argument, there are several weaknesses that negate his first point.

---

[60]Jeong Koo Jeon, *Covenant Theology: John Murray's and Meredith G. Kline's Response to the Historical Development of Federal Theology in Reformed Thought* (New York: University Press of America, 1999), pp. 186-87.

[61]Murray, *Collected Writings*, Vol. 2, pp. 55-56; so too Henry Morris, *The Genesis Record: A Scientific & Devotional Commentary on the Book of Beginnings* (Grand Rapids: Baker, 1976), p. 94.

First, Murray argues that Adam's place in the garden was founded upon grace rather than justice. Murray does not take into consideration the teaching of Scripture on the relationship between grace and works. Murray contends that Adam's presence in the garden was conditioned upon his obedience: 'The condition was obedience. Obedience was focused in compliance with the prohibition respecting the tree of the knowledge of good and evil.'[62] This means that Adam's presence in the garden was based upon a mixture of grace and merit – he had to be obedient but the results of his obedience would have been rewarded on the basis of grace rather than justice. Yet, what does Scripture say regarding the relationship between grace and works: 'If it is by grace, it is no longer on the basis of works; otherwise grace would no longer be grace' (Rom. 11:6). Contrary to Murray, Paul places grace and works in complete antithesis. Adam stands in the garden either by works or grace but not both.[63]

There is another consideration in Murray's argumentation that is defective on this point. Why is it not possible that Adam's obedience would have been judged by God's justice rather than grace? Sin has not yet entered the stage of history. If one carefully defines the nature of merit, or the reward for a performed work, then he can legitimately maintain that Adam had the possibility to merit a permanent place in the garden. One must define merit in terms of: (1) the fulfillment of the stipulations of a divinely sanctioned covenant; and (2) the measurement of merit in terms of that covenant.[64]

---

[62]Murray, *Collected Writings*, Vol. 2, p. 51.

[63]Elsewhere Murray acknowledges this very point but does not make the connection to Adam's state in the Garden: 'If grace is conditioned in any way by human performance or by the will of man impelling to action then grace ceases to be grace' (John Murray, *The Epistle to the Romans*, NICNT [rep.; Grand Rapids: Eerdmans, 1968], p. 70.

[64]Lee Irons, 'Redefining Merit: An Examination of Medieval Presuppositions in Covenant Theology,' in *Creator, Redeemer,*

God therefore offers Adam life or death based upon his obedience or disobedience, the terms of the covenant agreement. God does not deal with Adam as if he were his equal but in terms of the covenantal agreement. One may properly call Adam's state in the garden as one secured or lost by his own obedience or work.[65]

There is also an important connection between the work of the first and second Adam regarding the nature of merit. One point that Murray does not address in his

---

Consummator: A Festschrift for Meredith G. Kline, eds. Howard Griffith and John R. Muether (Greenville: Reformed Academic Press, 2000), p. 268. Irons points out that latent in the idea that Adam could not merit his place in the garden is the Roman Catholic theology of the Middle Ages, particularly the idea of condign and congruent merit. Murray relies upon Calvin's understanding of the covenant of grace (John Murray, *Collected Writings,* vol. 4, *Studies in Theology* [Edinburgh: Banner of Truth, 1982], pp. 218-19). What Murray does not treat, however, is Calvin's own understanding of Christ's merit. Calvin was influenced by the medieval nominalism of John Duns Scotus (c. 1266–1308) (see François Wendel, *Calvin: Origins and Developments of His Religious Thought,* trans. Philip Mairet [1950; Grand Rapids: Baker Books, 1997], pp. 228, 127-29). This is most evident when Calvin argues that Christ did not merit the salvation of the church on the basis of justice but of grace.

Calvin writes: 'In discussing Christ's merit, we do not consider the beginning of merit to be in him, but we go back to God's ordinance, the first cause. For God solely of his own good pleasure appointed him Mediator to obtain salvation for us. ... Apart from God's good pleasure Christ could not merit anything; but did so because he had been appointed to appease God's wrath with his sacrifice, and to blot out our transgressions with his obedience. To sum up: inasmuch as Christ's merit depends upon God's grace alone, which has ordained this manner of salvation for us, it is just as properly opposed to all human righteousness as God's grace is' (Calvin, *Institutes,* 2.17.1, p. 529).

The nominalist influence is clear – Christ's merit is only worth what value God assigns it. Christ's work, according to Calvin, is based in the Father's grace, not justice. To use a simple analogy, Calvin argues that Christ's merit is based, not upon a gold standard, but upon whatever value the government assigns it. Or, God graded Christ's work on a curve. This understanding, however, conflicts with Romans 11:6.

Despite the current popularity of Calvin's views in connection with the covenant, his views did not go unchecked. John Owen

criticism of the covenant of works is the parallel between Adam and Christ (Rom. 5:12-19).[66] As argued earlier, Adam is a type of Christ (Rom. 5:14). If Murray is correct, and Adam was judged on the basis of grace instead of justice, then the work of the second Adam is based not in terms of justice but grace. In this regard Kline notes that 'if meritorious works could not be predicated of Jesus Christ as second Adam, then obviously there would be no meritorious achievement to be imputed to his people

---

(1616–83) originally held to Calvin's views but later retracted them (see Carl R. Trueman, 'John Owen's *Dissertation on Divine Justice*: An Exercise in Christocentric Scholasticism,' *CTJ* 33/1 [1998], pp. 87-103; John Owen, *Dissertation on Divine Justice*, in *Works*, vol. 10, ed. William H. Goold [1850–53; Edinburgh: Banner of Truth, 1993], pp. 482-624). Inherent in Calvin's idea is that Christ's merit was not absolutely necessary if his role as mediator is merely one of appointment and his merit only has value in God's assignment of such. If Christ's merit was not judged based upon justice and absolute necessity, then God could have redeemed man by another means. Owen writes that Christ's merit is 'intimately connected with many, the most important articles of the Christian doctrine, concerning the attributes of God, the satisfaction of Christ, and the nature of sin, and of our obedience, and that it strikes its roots deep through almost the whole of theology, or the acknowledging of truth which is according to godliness' (*Dissertation*, p. 487). While one may certainly esteem Calvin, and by connection Murray, he must depart from them on this issue and side with Owen and the apostle Paul. Christ's merit was absolutely necessary and it was judged on the basis of God's justice, not grace.

[65]If one states that Adam's reward of eternal life is disproportionate with the required obedience, then the same must hold true for the punishment – it too must be disproportionate with Adam's disobedience. One must reject the idea that the reward is disproportionate with the work of obedience. Rather, both eternal life and death are the reward and punishment for Adam's obedience or disobedience *ex pacto*.

[66]Though Murray has orthodox conclusions in his interpretation of Romans 5:12-19 (see *Romans*, pp. 178-210), he analyzes the Adam and Christ connection in abstraction from the covenantal idea. Murray also does not deal with Romans 5:12-19 in his analysis of Adam's state in the garden (*Collected Writings*, Vol. 2, pp. 47-59). My colleague, Richard Gaffin, in conversation over this question called Murray 'a non-covenantal federalist', an apt description.

as the ground of their justification-approbation.'[67] Kline bases his point on Paul's statement: 'For as by the one man's disobedience the many were made sinners, so by the one man's obedience the many will be made righteous' (Rom. 5:19). Lee Irons succinctly notes that 'this parallelism between the two Adams demands that we see divine justice as the ground of both. For if the first Adam could not earn eternal life on the condition of meritorious obedience, then neither could the Last.'[68] Kline and Irons are not the only ones who have made this crucial observation. Others have also made the same connection, though the words of Hodge suffice:

> Perfect obedience was the condition of the covenant originally made with Adam. Had he retained his integrity he would have merited the promised blessing. For to him that works the reward is not of grace but of debt. In the same sense the work of Christ is the condition of the covenant of redemption. It was the meritorious ground, laying a foundation in justice for the fulfillment of the promises made to Him by the Father.[69]

There are also weaknesses with Murray's second criticism.

The term 'covenant' does not appear in connection with Adam

Murray argues that the term *covenant* does not appear in connection with Adam's state in the garden. Additionally, he also states that Hosea 6:7 need not be translated in a way to support the existence of the covenant of works. There are two considerations that negate Murray's propositions.

---

[67] Meredith G. Kline, *Kingdom Prologue: Genesis Foundations for a Covenantal Worldview* (Overland Park: Two Age Press, 2000), p. 108.

[68] Irons, 'Redefining Merit,' p. 268.

[69] Charles Hodge, *Systematic Theology* (1872–73; Grand Rapids: Eerdmans, 1993), pp. 364-65.

First, the absence of a term in connection with a doctrine does not necessarily negate the doctrine. Stated more technically, the formal absence of a term does not mean that it is materially nonexistent in a passage. Murray, for example, has no problem in calling God's redemptive dealings with man after the fall the 'covenant of grace', yet this term exists nowhere in Scripture. Murray correctly analyzes the substance of God's covenant with fallen man and concludes that it is one of grace. Similarly, looking at the creation of day and night in Genesis 1, there is no indication from the immediate context that God made a covenant; yet, when comparing Genesis 1:5 with Jeremiah 33:20 one finds that there is a covenantal relationship between God and the creation. In examining the creation of the first man and woman, the narrative states they are husband and wife, yet later Scripture identifies the marriage relationship as covenantal (Mal. 2:14).

Second, Murray offers no alternative interpretation on which to base his dismissal of Hosea 6:7. In the absence of any argumentation, it appears that Murray rejects Hosea 6:7 on dogmatic rather than exegetical grounds.

One comes to the third of Murray's objections.

Covenants are always redemptive

Murray contends that 'Scripture always uses the term covenant, when applied to God's administration to men, in reference to a provision that is redemptive or closely related to redemptive design.'[70] But is this the case? Are God's covenants with man exclusively redemptive in nature? If Murray is correct, then, yes, Adam could not be in a covenant in the garden – there

---

[70]Murray, *Collected Writings*, p. 49. This nature–creation and covenant–grace dualism is precisely the type of construction that some suggest, see Tim J. R. Trumper, 'Covenant Theology and Constructive Calvinism,' *WTJ* 64/2 (2002), pp. 387-404; cf. idem, 'Book Review: A. T. B. McGowan: *The Federal Theology of Thomas Boston*,' *WTJ* 62/1, pp. 153-57, esp. 156-57.

was no need for redemption prior to the fall. Murray's proposition is predicated on his idea that the essence of a covenant is embodied in the Noahic covenant. Murray takes a redemptive covenant and presumes that this is the only type of covenant. If sufficient evidence can be gathered to demonstrate that God created Adam in a covenantal context, Murray would be required to abandon his definition of a covenant. Sufficient evidence has been brought to the table to demonstrate that God's relationship with the creation and Adam was covenantal, foremost is the nomenclature of covenant ratification rather than initiation in the Noahic covenant (cf. Gen. 6:18; 15:18).

Summary
While respecting and admiring the theology of Murray at many points, one must acknowledge that his desire to reject the doctrine of the covenant of works is unscriptural. Murray's own self-avowed desire to revise, recast, and reconstruct Reformed theology concerning the covenant of works must be rejected.[71] While not wanting to adhere to the traditional interpretation merely for the sake of tradition, one must recognize that it is unwise to abandon the tradition without sufficient exegetical consideration and thought given to the theological implications. As Spkyman writes

> This covenantal deconstruction of Genesis 1–3 appears, moreover, to undermine Paul's teaching concerning the 'two Adams' in Romans 5. ... It also disrupts the close biblical connection between creation and redemption by reducing the idea of covenant to an exclusively salvific reality. One is then hard-pressed to avoid a dualist worldview, structured along nature-creation / grace-covenant lines. This Genesis approach

---

[71]See Murray, *Covenant*, p. 5; cf. Jeon, *Covenant Theology*, p. 186; J. V. Fesko, 'The Legacy of Old School Confession Subscription in the OPC,' *JETS* 46/4 (2003), pp. 673-98.

also lends support to the current tendency to find in the early Genesis record increasingly few matters of substantial importance for the faith-life and theology of the Christian community (for example, aversion to the idea of creation out of nothing, creation order, sabbath, and now covenant). It seriously interrupts the flow of covenant-kingdom continuity as a unifying theme running throughout biblical revelation. Contrastingly, therefore, Scripture still warrants the conclusion that God's 'new beginnings' with Noah, Abraham, Moses, and David represent successive renewals of the single covenant, reclaimed after the fall, but given originally and once for all time with creation.[72]

Covenantal deconstruction of Genesis 1–3 is unacceptable. It has been demonstrated that given the scriptural evidence – Genesis 1–3's covenant elements, Genesis 6:18, Jeremiah 33:20, and Hosea 6:7 – one may safely conclude that Adam, contrary to Murray's criticisms, was in relationship to God within a context of a covenant of works.

Conclusion

In the survey of the covenant of works this chapter has demonstrated that God gave Adam the responsibility of filling the earth with his image, extending the temple beyond the garden, subduing the earth by extending the order of the garden throughout the rest of the world, and extending God's rule through Adam's vicegerency. This was the work of Adam's covenant. There were, as in most covenants, conditions – the promise of death upon disobedience to God's command or life upon obedience. These covenant stipulations had visible signs, or sacraments – the trees of life and knowledge. Yet, as all sadly know, Adam did not choose obedience; instead he chose disobedience.[73]

---

[72]Spykman, *Reformational Theology*, p. 261.

[73]It is not known what amount of time Adam actually spent in the garden. Opinions vary from the rabbinic idea that Adam fell on the

As is clear from the above explanation of the covenant of works, Adam was a type, a foreshadow, of the one to come, the second Adam. It is the work of the eschatological Adam that our investigation now turns. For it is with a proper knowledge of protology, namely, patterns of the beginning, that enables one to understand properly christology and eschatology, or the end.

Before one may turn to the work of Christ, however, he must survey the rest of the Old Testament for other shadows and types of the second Adam. The rest of the Old Testament is laden with the protological imagery and patterns of Genesis 1–3.

---

tenth hour of day six (*Mid. Rabb.* Lev. 26.9; also Cassuto, *Genesis*, p. 164) to a period of several weeks (Morris, *Genesis*, p. 116). Though there is no way of knowing for certain, one might suggest that Adam was in the garden for a period close to forty days, which would parallel Christ's own period of temptation (Luke 4:2). There seem to be suggestions of this in some Jewish literature such as the *Life of Adam and Eve*: 'And Adam said to Eve, "You are not able to do so much as I; but do as much as you have strength for. I will spend forty days fasting" ' (6.1).

4

SHADOWS AND TYPES OF THE SECOND ADAM

Introduction

The study thus has established that God created man, Adam, in his image, placed him in the garden-temple, established a covenantal relationship with him, gave him the work of filling the earth with the image of God and extending the temple to the ends of the earth, and gave him a helpmate to accomplish this task. Adam chose to abandon his divinely granted vicegerency over the creation – he rebelled against God. Adam's rebellion, however, did not mean that God's intended goal for the creation was subverted. On the contrary, Genesis 3:15 states that God promised to send one who would crush the head of the serpent. The work of the one to come was not merely to destroy the serpent but, as will be evident from the rest of redemptive history, to take up the abandoned work of the first Adam. Throughout redemptive history until the advent of the second Adam, Jesus Christ, God establishes a series of covenants between himself and his chosen representative(s) that typify, or foreshadow, the person and work of the second Adam. One must therefore briefly survey the precursor types by an examination of the covenants that God makes prior to the advent of Christ.

The Noahic covenant

Subsequent to the fall of Adam, Scripture records a series of covenants throughout redemptive history. It is important to recognize that, in each of these covenants, God reissues the mandate of the first covenant with Adam. There are several elements found in God's covenant with Adam: (1) spreading the image of God throughout the earth; (2) extending the temple to the ends of the earth; (3) exercising dominion over the earth through elements 1 and 2; and (4) accomplishing this task with the assistance of a helpmate. The first mention of the word *covenant* is made in connection with God's dealings with Noah. One should not, as is common among dispensational theologians, believe that God has entered into a covenantal relationship with Noah that has no precedent in the covenant with Adam.[1] A close examination of the covenants with Adam and Noah reveal striking similarities between the two. The parallels between the two are evident in the dominion mandate that is given to Adam and to Noah:

Adam (Gen. 1:28)	**Noah (Gen. 9:1-3)**
And God blessed them. And God said to them, 'Be fruitful and multiply and fill the earth and subdue it and have dominion over the fish of the sea and over the birds of the heavens and over every living thing that moves on the earth.'	And God blessed Noah and his sons and said to them, 'Be fruitful and multiply and fill the earth. The fear of you and the dread of you shall be upon every beast of the earth and upon every bird of the heavens, upon everything that creeps on the ground and all the fish of the sea. Into your hand they are delivered. Every moving thing that lives shall be food for you. And as I gave you the green plants, I give you everything.'

---

[1]Charles Ryrie, *Dispensationalism Today* (1965; Chicago: Moody Press, 1970), pp. 52-53.

God assigns the same tasks to Noah as he did to Adam.[2] The same elements are present: (1) spreading the image of God throughout the earth (Gen. 9.7); (2) though access to the garden-temple has been barred due to its destruction in the flood, the worship of God was likewise to be spread throughout the earth; (3) dominion of the earth is accomplished via means 1 and 2; and (4) Noah accomplishes this task through his offspring, the fruit of the union between Noah and his helpmate.

The parallels between the initial creation and the re-emergence of the creation after the deluge are striking. Along these lines Warren Gage comments that

> the ordering of the present heavens and earth out of the chaotic overthrow of the ancient world recorded in Genesis 8 parallels the original creation account of Genesis 1. In both chapters the theological narrative moves from the display of divine work to the account of divine rest. In Genesis 8.1 God brings about a wind to pass over the waters of the flood which like the waters of original chaos (Gen. 1.2), cover the earth (Gen. 7.18-19). The emergence of the dry land and the bringing forth of vegetation (Gen. 1.12) find a mirror image in the olive leaf brought to Noah, which is taken as a token of the emergence of dry land (Gen. 8.11). Noah's sabbatical

---

[2]W. J. Dumbrell, *Covenant and Creation: A Theology of the Old Testament Covenants* (1984; Carlisle: Paternoster, 2002), p. 33. Commentators are in virtual agreement regarding the republication of the dominion mandate (Nahum Sarna, *Genesis*, JPSTC [Phildelphia: JPS, 1989] p. 60; Hermann Gunkel, *Genesis*, trans. Mark E. Biddle [Macon: Mercer UP, 1997], p. 148; Claus Westermann, *Genesis 1-11*, trans. John J. Scullion [Minneapolis: Fortress, 1994], p. 462; Gerhard von Rad, *Genesis*, OTL [Philadelphia: Westminster, 1972], p. 131; H. C. Leupold, *Exposition of Genesis*, vol. 1 [Grand Rapids: Baker, 1942], pp. 327-28; Henry Morris, *The Genesis Record: A Scientific and Devotional Commentary on the Book of Beginnings* [Grand Rapids: Baker, 1976], pp. 221-22, 236-37; Derek Kidner, *Genesis*, TOTC [Downers Grove: Intervarsity, 1967], p. 100; Gordon J. Wenham, *Genesis 1-15*, WBC, vol. 1 [Dallas: Word, 1989], p. 192; John Walton, *Genesis*, NIVAC [Grand Rapids: Zondervan, 2001], p. 341).

pattern in sending of the dove suggests that God alone, who created the first world in six days, can deliver the earth from such a catastrophe. The sabbath rest of God at the conclusion of the original creation ('and He rested,' וַיִּשְׁבֹּת [wayyišbōṭ], Gen. 2.2) finds correspondence in the sacrificial rest of God after the new creation is completed ('and the Lord smelled the aroma of rest,' הַנִּיחֹחַ רֵיחַ [rêªḥ hannîḥōªḥ]; Gen. 8.21).[3]

The parallels between the initial creation and post-deluge creation mean that God started over with Noah as a new Adam, of sorts, giving to Noah the same covenantal tasks as the first.[4] This subsequent Adam, however, could not fulfill the requirements set before him in the covenant. Shortly after the beginning of the new creation, that is, the post-flood world, Noah sinned in circumstances reminiscent of the fall.

Adam fell in a garden (Gen. 3:1) whereas Noah sinned in a vineyard (Gen. 9:20), a garden-like setting. Noah drank from the fruit of the vine while Adam ate of the fruit of a tree (Gen. 9:20; 3:2). Just as Adam was upright and created in the image of God, so too Noah was 'a righteous man, blameless in his generation' (Gen. 6:9a). Noah even 'walked with God,' a relationship reminiscent of that of Adam with whom God walked in the garden in the cool of the day (cf. Gen. 3:8; 6:9b). Yet despite Noah's rectitude, he nonetheless became drunk and exposed himself.[5] Noah's nakedness was covered by his sons (Gen. 9:23) as Adam's sin was covered by God

---

[3]Warren Austin Gage, *The Gospel of Genesis: Studies in Protology and Eschatology* (Eugene: Wipf & Stock, 1984), pp. 10-11.

[4]Though not a primary focus of the study, there is the strong possibility that Noah's ark was itself a temple. For example, the LXX translates the term κιβωτός (kibōtos), which is also the term used for the ark of the covenant, when in the Hebrew they are two different terms. The ark had three stories, just like Israel's tabernacle and temple. Similarly, the only other occurrence of detailed architectural plans in the Old Testament are for the tabernacle and temple (See G. K. Beale, 'Garden Temple,' *Kerux* 18/2 [2003], p. 31, n. 80).

[5]Wenham, *Genesis*, p. 199.

(Gen. 3:21).[6] In fact, the Scriptures associate nakedness and inebriation with shame and loss of dignity just as in the fall of Adam and Eve (cf. Hab. 2:15; Lam. 4:21; Gen. 3:7, 21).[7] Lastly, in both accounts the narrative moves from the sin of the fathers to an ensuing blessing and cursing of the seed.[8] Despite this new Adam, the cleansing of the creation, the republication of the dominion mandate with its constituent elements, there is the looming specter of sin. This Adam, that is Noah, cannot fulfill the requirements of the covenant of works. The people of God must therefore look beyond Noah, to another Adam.

The Abrahamic covenant

God continues his redemptive activity in his dealings with the patriarch of the Israelites, Abraham. What many, if not all, commentators readily acknowledge is that God made a covenant with Abraham. The specifics of this covenant appear in Genesis 12:1ff and 17:1ff. Yet some commentators fail to recognize the continuity between the Adamic and Abrahamic covenants.[9]

Recall the constituent elements of the Abrahamic covenant. First, God promised to multiply Abraham exceedingly (Gen. 17:2). More specifically, the goal of God's covenant with Abraham is that he would be the 'father of a multitude of nations' (Gen. 17:4). In fact, God changes his name from Abram to Abraham, which means 'father of a multitude of nations' (Gen. 12:1-3; 17:5). God's blessing is basically that of a king, similar to the role of Adam who was the vicegerent over the creation (2 Sam. 7:9; Ps. 72:17).[10] The goal of the Abrahamic

---

[6]Cf. Walton, *Genesis*, pp. 346-47; Kidner, *Genesis*, p. 103.

[7]Sarna, *Genesis*, p. 65.

[8]Gage, *Gospel of Genesis*, p. 12. For an in-depth study of the Adam and Noah parallels see Devora Steinmetz, 'Vineyard, Farm, and Garden: The Drunkenness of Noah in the Context of Primeval History,' *JBL* 113/2 (1994), pp. 193-207.

[9]E.g. Ryrie, *Dispensationalism*, pp. 60-61.

[10]Wenham, *Genesis*, p. 275.

covenant is that the blessings of this covenant are eventually supposed to spread to the ends of the earth. Global expansion is the import of the phrase: 'In you all the families of the earth shall be blessed' (Gen. 12:3).[11] Abraham embarked on this aspect of his covenantal responsibilities with the assistance of Sarah, his helpmate, paralleling the work of the first Adam and the dominion mandate – to spread the image and worship of God to the ends of the earth. Just as Adam was given a geographic center of gravity from which to carry out his labors, so too Abraham is given the land of Canaan – a land of promise (Gen. 17:8).[12] Moreover, Adam was to worship God in the archetypal temple, so too Abraham constructed temples, of sorts.

When Abraham arrived in the promised land he commemorated the event by building an altar and worshiping God (Gen. 12:7). Abraham built an altar because God appeared to him, the first recorded theophany to a patriarch (cf. Gen. 17:1; 18:1; 26:2, 24; 35:9; 48:3). Gordon Wenham comments that God's appearance 'in turn foreshadows his appearances at Sinai and in the tabernacle (Exod. 3:2, 16; 16:10; Lev. 9:4)'.[13] Concerning the patriarchal theophanies and altar worship Geerhardus Vos writes:

> The theophany marks the first step toward the return of primitive, normal intercourse. With respect to the future, the theophany presents the renewal of the paradise-condition and as such presages a full future paradise. It points to the new world. ... An approach

---

[11]Wenham, *Genesis*, p. 278. According to rabbinic interpretation Abraham was the one who was supposed to 'set things right,' in other words undo the failed work of Adam (*Mid. Rabb.* Gen. 14.6).

[12]The Qumran community uses language that is reminiscent of Eden in describing the promised land: 'A land of brooks of water, [of fountains and springs, flowing forth in val]leys and hills, and land of wheat and barley, [of vines and fig trees and pomegranates, a land of olive trees and] honey' (4Q378 II).

[13]Wenham, *Genesis*, p. 279.

toward permanent nearness is made by the building of altars, which are revisited places that God might frequent. All this prepares for the permanent divine indwelling. Canaan prefigures the eschatological state of Israel. It is the land flowing with milk and honey; i.e. typical of paradise. Note that Canaan was afterwards the scene of the highest permanent theophany of the Old Testament (i.e. the temple) and therefore typical of the final consummate state of the theocracy.[14]

Abraham's altar, therefore, hearkens back to God's initial appearances to Adam in the garden-temple.[15] There is confirmation of this understanding in the significance of an altar.

The Hebrew word for *altar*, מִזְבֵּחַ (mizbēᵃḥ) has in its root the verb *sacrifice*, זָבַח (zéḇaḥ).[16] This means that an altar was the place where a sacrifice was offered; in other words, priestly activity was conducted at these sites. It was also a place where God chose to meet with his people (Gen. 22:14; Exod. 20:24; Judg. 13:16; 1 Kings 3:15).[17] One may therefore legitimately conclude that these altars were miniature temple sites.[18] Scripture records that Cain and Abel were the first ones to build altars (Gen. 4:3-4), though it is likely that this was first done by Adam and Eve.[19] Noah also constructed such an altar (Gen. 8:20). Abraham constructed altars in various locations: Shechem, Bethel, Ai, and Moriah (Gen. 12:8;

---

[14]Geerhardus Vos, *Eschatology of the Old Testament*, ed. James T. Dennison (Phillipsburg: P & R, 2001), pp. 85-86.

[15]Rabbinic interpreters later identified the patriarchal altar sites as the site of the temple (see *Mid. Rabb.* Gen. 56.10; 69.7; also Beale, 'Garden Temple,' p. 24, n. 64).

[16]Richard E. Averbeck, 'מִזְבֵּחַ' in NIDOTTE, vol. 2, pp. 888-908; idem, 'זבח' in NIDOTTE, vol. 1, pp. 1066-73.

[17]Tremper Longman, *Immanuel in Our Place: Seeing Christ in Israel's Worship* (Phillipsburg: P & R, 2001), pp. 16-17; Wenham, *Genesis*, p. 280.

[18]Richard E. Averbeck, 'Offerings and Sacrifices,' in NIDOTTE, vol. 4, p. 1008.

[19]Averbeck, 'מִזְבֵּחַ' in NIDOTTE, vol. 2, p. 889.

13:4, 18; 22:9); the landscape of the promised land was dotted with altars. Moreover, Abraham's descendants continued the practice of altar construction: Isaac at Beersheba (Gen. 26:25); Jacob at Luz (Gen. 35:7); and even Moses at Rephidim and Sinai (Exod. 17:15; 24:4).[20] There are two important factors that must be noted regarding these altars.

First, while perhaps not in every case, Abraham constructed these altars atop mountains (Gen. 12:8; 22:9, 14). Jacob built an altar at Luz, or Bethel, because it was 'the gate of heaven' (Gen. 28:17-19; 35:7), which also lies in the mountains.[21] Second, Abraham typically built his altars in the midst of tree groves.[22] Abraham's first altar was built in Shechem, by the 'oak of Moreh' (Gen. 12:6). Abraham also dwelled 'by oaks of Mamre, which are at Hebron, and there he built an altar to the LORD' (Gen. 13:18). That Abraham and his descendants built altars on mountaintops in the midst of tree groves is of course reminiscent of the garden-temple – the garden of Eden.[23]

God's covenant with Abraham provides continuity with the covenant made with Adam. It has the same goals and many of the same features. Along these lines John Walton observes that Genesis 'chapters 1 and 9 feature God's blessing and establish the areas of blessing as the provision of offspring and food. Here it is no surprise that the blessing God offers concerns

---

[20]Wenham, *Genesis*, p. 280.

[21]O. Palmer Robertson, *Understanding the Land of the Bible: A Biblical-Theological Guide* (Phillipsburg: P & R, 1996), p. 42.

[22]One must also recognize that despite the fact that God constructed the temple, the official location of where he was to be worshiped, the Israelites – informed by the ANE religions around them, whose practices likely echoed the practices of Adam in the garden, though now distorted by the fall – continued to worship on high ground in the midst of trees (Longman, *Immanuel in Our Place*, p. 21). See Lev. 26:30; Num. 33:52; Deut. 12:2; 1 Kings 14:23; 2 Chron. 28:4. The Qumran community believed the altars and 'sacred trees' had to be destroyed (2QT = 2Q19, 20).

[23]Longman, *Immanuel in Our Place*, p. 21.

bringing Abram into a land (which will be a fertile land where they can grow their crops and prosper) and making an abundant family spring up from him.'[24] Additionally, parallels arise in other parts of Scripture. Language reminiscent of the creation narrative emerges in connection with God's dealings with Abraham. Just as God called the creation into existence out of nothing (Gen. 1:1-3; Heb. 11:1), which ultimately resulted in the creation of Adam, the first covenantal head charged with carrying out the labor of the covenant of works, so too God called Abraham into existence: 'As it is written, "I have made you the father of many nations" – in the presence of the God in whom he believed, who gives life to the dead and calls into existence the things that do not exist' (Rom. 4:17).[25] Paul's statement concerns God's ability to create *ex nihilo*, something he did both at the creation and now in types that foreshadow the new creation (cf. Isa. 41:4; 48:13; 2 Macc. 7:28).[26] In this regard James Dunn notes that

> equally important is the fact that this is a description of God the creator. It is precisely as creator that he is the life-giver and life-sustainer (Neh. 9:6; *Jos. As.* 8.9). Of course the thought here is of God who gives life to the dead, but in this way of speaking about God the eschatological manifestation of his life-giving power is simply the supreme example of his creative power – the

---

[24]Walton, *Genesis*, p. 392.

[25]Dumbrell, *Covenant*, p. 58.

[26]C. E. B. Cranfield, *Romans*, ICC, vol. 1 (1975; Edinburgh: T & T Clark, 2001), p. 244; similarly Charles Hodge, *Romans* (1835; Edinburgh: Banner of Truth, 1989), p. 124; James D. G. Dunn, *Romans*, WBC, vol. 38a (Dallas: Word, 1988), p. 218; Herman Ridderbos, *Paul: An Outline of His Theology*, trans. John Richard de Witt (1975; Grand Rapids: Eerdmans, 1997), p. 351; John Calvin, *Romans and Thessalonians*, CNTC (1960; Grand Rapids: Eerdmans, 1995), p. 96; cf. John Murray, *Romans*, NICNT (1959; Grand Rapids: Eerdmans, 1968), pp. 146-47; Douglas Moo, *Romans*, NICNT (Grand Rapids: Eerdmans, 1996), pp. 281-82; Thomas Schreiner, *Romans*, BECNT (Grand Rapids: Baker Books, 1998), p. 237.

same creative power which first gave life will have the final say over that which seems most to threaten the life he gave us in the beginning.[27]

In other words, one of the major themes of protology, God as creator, is intimately connected with redemption, or soteriology, and eschatology. All of these things point to an important but seldom noticed connection between the first Adam and Abraham. N. T. Wright observes that in Abraham's call, circumcision, the offering of Isaac and transition from Abraham to Isaac and Jacob, that

> the narrative quietly insists that Abraham and his progeny inherit the role of Adam and Eve. There are, interestingly, two differences which emerge in the shape of this role. The command ('be fruitful ...') has turned into a promise ('I will make you fruitful ...'), and possession of the land of Canaan, together with supremacy over enemies, has taken the place of Adam's dominion over nature.[28]

Once again, the patterns of protology set a trajectory for the patterns revealed throughout redemptive history. The same protological elements surface in the subsequent covenant with Israel.

The Mosaic covenant

In the Mosaic covenant there are a myriad of protological elements scattered throughout the Pentateuch. It must first be recognized that the Mosaic covenant does not arise *de novo* in the Old Testament but that it has its roots in the Abrahamic covenant (Exod. 2:24; 3:6).[29] The parallels

[27]Dunn, *Romans*, pp. 236-37.

[28]N. T. Wright, *The New Testament and the People of God* (Philadelphia: Fortress, 1992), p. 263; also Dumbrell, *Covenant*, pp. 63-68; similarly C. K. Barrett, *From First Adam to Last* (London: Adam & Charles Black, 1962), p. 35.

[29]O. Palmer Robertson, *The Christ of the Covenants* (Phillipsburg: P & R, 1980), pp. 215-18; Dumbrell, *Covenant*, p. 87; cf. contra Ryrie, *Dispensationalism*, pp. 53-54.

between the garden-temple and the desert tabernacle have already been noted: the seven days of creation and the seven speeches surrounding the construction of the tabernacle; the presence of ornamental trees, precious stones and metal; the menorah as a copy of the tree of life; the veil of the holy of holies with the embroidered cherubim; God walking in the garden and walking about in the tabernacle; God was served by Adam, an archetypal Levite, as he was served by the Levites, and meeting with God atop a mountain, Mount Sinai (Exod. 19:2).[30] Beyond these parallels there are further continuities between the covenant of works with Adam, particularly its goals, and the Mosaic covenant with Israel.

Recall that Adam was God's son (Luke 3:38); this is also true of Israel: 'Israel is my firstborn son' (Exod. 4:22; cf. Hos. 11:1). God placed Adam in the garden, which was a source of sustenance and the location of the temple, and so too God placed Israel, his son, in a land flowing with milk and honey (Exod. 13:5). The spies who reconnoitered the promised land brought back the fruit of the land (Num. 13:27). G. K. Beale notes that 'Israel's land is explicitly compared to the Garden of Eden (see Gen. 13:10; Isa. 51:3; Ezek. 36:35; 47:12; Joel 2.3) and is portrayed as very fruitful in order to heighten the correspondence to Eden (cf. Deut. 8:7-10; 11:8-17; Ezek. 47:1-12).'[31] The promised land was also the ultimate resting place of the once ambulatory desert tabernacle – the place where Israel met with, served, and offered sacrifices to God. When the ultimate goals of the covenant made with Israel are considered, the same protological elements reappear. Consider that Israel was to be a kingdom of priests (Exod. 19:6). James Durham writes that 'Israel as a "kingdom of priests" is Israel committed to the extension throughout the world of the

---

[30]Longman, *Immanuel*, p. 35.
[31]Beale, 'Garden Temple,' p. 44.

ministry of Yahweh's Presence.'[32] Israel was to take the redemptive knowledge of God to the ends of the earth in the same way that Adam was to spread the image and worship of God throughout the earth (Isa. 49:6).

Considering that Israel, God's son, was placed in the land – a source of sustenance and the location of God's presence – points to the idea that Israel was expected to perform essentially the same functions intended for Adam. As the dominion mandate was reissued to Noah, Israel too received a version of the mandate. Leviticus 26:6-12 alludes to Genesis 1:28 in direct connection to the completion of the tabernacle in Israel's midst and echoes Genesis 9:3 and the fear that the animals were to have of man once again:

> I will give peace in the land, and you shall lie down, and none shall make you afraid. And I will remove harmful beasts from the land, and the sword shall not go through your land. ... I will turn to you and make you fruitful and multiply you and will confirm my covenant with you. ... I will make my dwelling among you, and my soul shall not abhor you. And I will walk among you and will be your God, and you shall be my people.

In this connection, Wright notes that 'if Abraham and his family are understood as the creator's means of dealing with the sin of Adam, and hence with the evil in the world, Israel herself becomes the true Adamic humanity.'[33] He goes on to write that not only does this theme run through the Pentateuch, but that it emerges in the prophets: 'The prophets call Israel to be the people through whom YHWH will act in relation to the whole world. The point of this, in terms (for the moment) of Israel's own role, is that she is taking the place – under God and over the world – which according to the Genesis

---

[32]John I. Durham, *Exodus*, WBC, vol. 3 (Dallas: Word, 1987), p. 263.

[33]Wright, *People of God*, p. 262.

picture was the place of Adam' (Isa. 2:2-5; 42:6; 49:6; 51:4; Mic. 4:1-5; Ezek. 40–47, esp. 47:7-12; Zeph. 3:20; Zech. 14:8-19).[34] These are not the only parallels between Adam and Israel.

Just as Adam had blessings and curses specified in his covenant, so too Israel had its own covenant blessings and curses:

> Because you listen to these rules and keep and do them, the LORD your God will keep with you the covenant and the steadfast love that he swore to your fathers. He will love you, bless you, and multiply you. ... And if you forget the LORD your God and go after other gods and serve them and worship them, I solemnly warn you today that you shall surely perish (Deut. 7:12-13; 8:19).

One should note the similarities between the blessings and curses of the covenant of works and the stipulations of the Mosaic covenant. In this regard Vos notes how

> the abode of Israel in Canaan typified the heavenly, perfected state of God's people. Under these circumstances the ideal of absolute conformity to God's law of legal holiness had to be upheld. Even though they were not able to keep this law in the Pauline, spiritual sense, yea, even though they were unable to keep it externally and ritually, the requirement could not be lowered. When apostasy on a general scale took place, they could not remain in the promised land. When they disqualified themselves for typifying the state of holiness, they *ispso facto* disqualified themselves for typifying that of blessedness, and had to go into captivity.[35]

In other words, Israel was supposed to dwell in this garden-like land, worship and serve God, multiply the image of God and worship of him throughout the

---

[34]Wright, *People of God*, p. 264.

[35]Geerhardus Vos, *Biblical Theology: Old and New Testaments* (1948; Edinburgh: Banner of Truth, 1996), p. 127.

earth, and upon the completion of their work enter the eternal Sabbath rest of God. Of course, Israel did not do this and, like Adam, was ejected out of the garden-like land and the temple was destroyed. Because of the obvious parallels between Adam in the garden and Israel in the promised land, some scholars argue that the Mosaic covenant is a repetition of the covenant of works, though not in the sense that the Israelites could somehow merit their salvation.[36] At the level of typology, the covenant of works is republished in the Mosaic covenant, which showcases Israel's inability to fulfill the broken covenant of works and points to the need of the true second Adam. The republication idea finds historic precedence from within the Reformed tradition in the Westminster Confession, which states that 'God gave to Adam a law, as a covenant of works' (19.1). The divines then go on to say that, 'This law, after his fall, continued to be a perfect rule of righteousness; and, as such, was delivered by God upon Mount Sinai, in ten commandments, and written in two tables' (19.2). Similarly, in the Shorter Catechism (Question 40) the divines ask, 'What did God at first reveal to man for the rule of his obedience?,' to which they answer: 'The rule which God at first revealed to man for his obedience, was the moral law.' The next question states, 'Wherein is the moral law summarily comprehended?' The divines again answer, 'The moral law is summarily comprehended in

---

[36]Charles Hodge, *1 & 2 Corinthians* (1857-59; Edinburgh: Banner of Truth, 1994), pp. 432-34; James Buchanan, *The Doctrine of Justification* (1867; Edinburgh: Banner of Truth, 1991), pp. 38-39; Meredith Kline, *Kingdom Prologue: Genesis Foundations for a Covenantal Worldview* (Overland Park: Two Age Press, 2000), p. 110. Though Murray disagrees with this construction, it is one that he recognizes has 'exercised a profound influence upon the history' of the development of the relationship of the Mosaic covenant to the covenant of grace (John Murray, *Collected Writings*, 4 vols. [1977; Edinburgh: Banner of Truth, 1996], vol. 2, p. 50; idem, *Principles of Conduct: Aspects of Biblical Ethics* [1957; Grand Rapids: Eerdmans, 2001], p. 196).

the Ten Commandments.' The Westminster Standards, then, have long recognized the republication of the covenant of works in the Mosaic covenant.[37] There are yet further connections between the Mosaic covenant and the themes and patterns of protology.

There are significant parallels surrounding the Israelite exodus from Egypt and the creation.[38] In the initial creation, the Holy Spirit, like a bird, hovers, מְרַחֶפֶת (məraḥépeṭ), over the face of the primeval chaotic waters (Gen. 1:2). The same avian imagery is connected to God's superintendence of Israel in their wilderness wanderings: 'He found him in a desert land.... As an eagle stirs up its nest, hovers [יְרַחֵף / yəraḥēp̄] over its young, spreading out its wings, taking them up, carrying them on its wings' (Deut. 32:10-11; NKJ). Scholars have connected the cloud that accompanied the Israelites on the exodus with the Holy Spirit of Genesis 1:2 (cf. Hag. 2:5).[39] Additionally, it may be noted that in the same way in which the Holy Spirit superintended the creation, so too he superintended the construction of the tabernacle (Exod. 31:2-3), which was a reproduction of not only the cosmic temple of God, the creation, but also the microcosmic archetypal temple of God, the

---

[37]Contra D. Patrick Ramsey, 'In Defense of Moses: A Confessional Critique of Kline and Karlberg,' *WTJ* 66/2 (2004), pp. 394-95; cf. Francis R. Beattie, *The Presbyterian Standards* (rep.; Greenville: Southern Presbyterian Press, 1997), pp. 246-50; A. A. Hodge, *The Confession of Faith* (rep.; Edinburgh: Banner of Truth), pp. 251-52; Robert Shaw, *An Exposition of the Westminster Confession of Faith* (1845; Fearn: Christian Focus, 1998), p. 243.

[38]N. A. Dahl, 'Christ, Creation and the Church,' in *The Background of the New Testament and Its Eschatology*, eds. W. D. Davies and D. Daube (Cambridge: Cambridge University Press, 1956), p. 425. Barrett points out that, 'Under Moses an act of deliverance took place which Old Testament writers themselves compared with the mythological drama in which God defeated the forces of chaos, and so established his creation' (Barrett, *First Adam to Last*, p. 93). See, e.g. 'Was it not you who cut Rahab in pieces, that pierced the dragon?' (Isa. 51:9; cf. Ps. 89:10).

[39]Meredith Kline, *Images of the Spirit* (Eugene: Wipf & Stock, 1998), p. 19; cf. DSS 4Q504-6 fr. 6.

garden.[40] In fact, the phrase רוּחַ אֱלֹהִים (rûᵃḥ ʾĕlōhîm), 'Spirit of God,' is used in only three other places in Scripture (Gen. 1:2; 41:38; Num. 24:2). This phrase is used twice in connection with the construction of the tabernacle (Exod. 31:3; 35:31), which 'implies that the creative force present at creation is likewise present in the building of the tabernacle'.[41] In addition to these protological connections to the Holy Spirit, there are also further connections related to the primeval waters and Israel.

Recall that the dry land first emerged out of the miry depths of the primeval chaotic waters (Gen. 1:9-13). On dry land the creation subsequently flourished, giving animals and man a place upon which they could exist. In other words, the creation emerged from the primeval waters. This reality was repeated with the judgment and re-creation of the deluge. Once again the dry land, the creation, emerged from the waters of the deluge (Gen. 8:13). Interestingly, scholars point to the connection between the Holy Spirit, רוּחַ (rûᵃḥ), hovering over the primeval waters (Gen. 1:2), the wind, רוּחַ (rûᵃḥ), that God used to cause the waters to recede (Gen. 8:1), and Noah sending a dove, an avian symbolic representation of the Holy Spirit, to hover and fly over the deluged creation in search of dry land (Gen. 8:8-12; cf. John 1:32).[42] At each point in redemptive history one finds the work of the Holy Spirit conveyed in terms of avian imagery, hovering like a bird over the primeval waters, a dove over the flood waters, or hovering over Israel like a bird at the exodus. Yet, the parallels between protology and Israel's creation grow even stronger.

---

[40]Longman, *Immanuel*, p. 35; Vern S. Poythress, *The Shadow of Christ in the Law of Moses* (Phillipsburg: P & R, 1991), pp. 13-18.

[41]Peter Enns, *Exodus*, NIVAC (Grand Rapids: Zondervan, 2000), p. 543 n. 47; also Walter Brueggemann, *Theology of the Old Testament* (Minneapolis: Fortress, 1997), p. 533. Rabbinic interpreters also make the connection between the Spirit of God superintending the creation of the cosmos and the tabernacle (see *Mid. Rabb.* Exo. 48.4).

[42]Gage, *Gospel*, pp. 10-11.

In similar fashion Israel, as a nation, was born or created from the waters – the waters of the Red Sea (Exod. 14:21-23). In this regard Gage comments:

> By introducing the scriptural history of Israel with Genesis, Moses identifies Yahweh of the exodus with Elohim of Creation. Consequently the exodus-eisodus history of the hexateuch is so structured as to be a redemptive reenactment of creation. The redemptive creation of Israel at the sea is cast in the same narrative style of original creation as the pillar of divine presence brings light into darkness (Exod. 13:21, cf. the first creative day), the waters are divided (Exod. 14:21; cf. the second creative day), and the dry land emerges (Exod. 14:29, cf. the third creative day). In the wilderness the superintending care of God at the creation of Israel is paralleled to the Spirit hovering over the waters of chaos (cf. רחף in Gen. 1:2 and Deut. 32:11), while the exodus event culminates in the eisodus into the paradisical Canaan, a redemptive correlative to the creative sabbath (cf. Heb. 4:3-10).[43]

The patterns of protology do not, therefore, drift into the background of redemptive history. Rather, they are embossed across its entire narrative. Gage raises one last connection between protology and the Mosaic covenant that deserves attention, namely, the Sabbath.

One of the re-emerging protological patterns is that of the Sabbath. Recall that God took his Sabbath rest at the conclusion of his creative labors (Gen. 2:2-3). Not only did God rest from his own labors but Adam, following a successful conclusion of his period of probation, was supposed to enter the Sabbath rest of God. Vos notes that 'the so-called "Covenant of Works" was nothing but an embodiment of the Sabbatical principle. Had its probation been successful, then the sacramental Sabbath would have passed over into the reality it typified, and

---

[43]Gage, *Gospel*, pp. 20-21.

the entire subsequent course of the history of the race would have been radically different.[44] With each passing Sabbath, Adam would have rested from his own labors, the labors of the covenant of works, until he successfully completed his assigned mandate. Upon its completion, he would have entered into the eternal Sabbath rest of God. The recurring Sabbath was to function as an eschatological sign – a symbol of the goal of creation even in the pre-fall world. Vos writes that 'the Sabbath is an expression of the eschatological principle on which the life of humanity has been constructed'.[45] Now, it is this specific Sabbath principle, this protological pattern, that is carried over in the Mosaic covenant.

The Sabbath rest of Genesis 2:2-3 serves essentially the same function for Israel as it did for Adam, though there is a slight twist: 'Above all you shall keep my Sabbaths, for this is a sign between me and you throughout your generations, that you may know that I, the LORD, sanctify you' (Exod. 31:13). One should notice that Adam in his pre-fall state was in no need of sanctification. Adam's Sabbath represented an attainable eschatological goal based upon his labors within the covenant of works. Israel, however, stands in a redemptive relationship with God. Consequently, the Sabbath is a reminder to them that it is God who ultimately brings about their redemption. This aspect of the Mosaic covenant will be explored below.

There is a second aspect attached to the Sabbath, one that appeals directly to protology: 'It is a sign forever between me and the people of Israel that in six days the LORD made heaven and earth, and on the seventh day he rested and was refreshed' (Exod. 31:17; cf. 20:8-11). The Sabbath is not only a sign of God's redemptive activity at work in the midst of Israel, but it is also a sign of God's lordship over creation and of his eternal rest, which still remains as the eschatological

---

[44]Vos, *Biblical Theology*, p. 140.
[45]Vos, *Biblical Theology*, p. 140.

goal for the creation.[46] In this case, it also serves as an eschatological sign for Israel; each Sabbath they rest from their own labors of fulfilling the dominion mandate to look forward to the day when they will complete their labors and enter God's eternal Sabbath rest. Dumbrell notes that 'on the sabbath, therefore, Israel is to reflect upon the question of ultimate purposes for herself as a nation, and for the world over which she is set. For in pointing back to the creation, the sabbath points also to what is yet to be, to the final destiny to which all creation is moving.'[47] It must be said that the institution of the Sabbath, not only at Sinai (Exod. 20:8-11) but also at the completion of the tabernacle instructions (Exod. 31:12ff), and the account of the construction of the tabernacle (Exod. 35:1ff), demonstrates the intimate connection between the Sabbath rest of God in the creation and the construction of the archetypal temple, the garden, and its successor, the tabernacle.[48] The Sabbath proves the irrefragable connection between protology and eschatology.

The Davidic covenant

When one explores the Davidic covenant, he finds that there are connections in God's dealings with King David that are rooted in protology, particularly in the construction of the temple, God's dwelling place. God makes a covenant with David and promises to place one of his heirs on the throne of Israel from which this heir would rule, 'build a house' for God's name, God would be his father, and the heir would be a son to him (2 Sam. 7.13-14).[49] Once again there are similar themes that echo the initial creation: a king will rule, who is

---

[46]Brevard S. Childs, *The Book of Exodus*, OTL (1974; Louisville: Westminster, 1976), p. 542.

[47]Dumbrell, *Covenant*, p. 35.

[48]Childs, *Exodus*, p. 541.

[49]A. A. Anderson, *2 Samuel*, WBC, vol. 11 (Dallas: Word, 1989), p. 122.

called God's son, and will build God's dwelling place, a temple. Adam was God's son, ruled the creation, and was supposed to extend the garden-temple to the ends of the earth. We see temple-building connected with King David quite prominently in the first book of Chronicles.

Beale explains that in David's preparatory actions to build the temple in Jerusalem, which would ultimately be accomplished by his son, Solomon, that David, like the patriarchs, Abraham, Isaac, and Jacob, built an altar. Altar-building, as demonstrated above, is priestly activity and is tied to God's dwelling places, or temples. Beale points out that

1. David begins the preparations on a mountain (Mount Moriah)
2. He experiences a theophany (he sees 'the angel of the LORD'; 1 Chron. 21:16; 2 Chron. 3:1).
3. At this location David 'built an altar to the LORD' and offered sacrifices (1 Chron. 21:26).
4. David calls the place 'the house of the LORD God' (1 Chron. 22:1) because it is the site of Israel's future temple (1 Chron. 22; 2 Chron. 3:1).[50]

Here in David's preparations one continues to see protological elements – priestly activity atop a mountain, the appearance of God, God's dwelling place, a temple, all performed by a king, one with whom God is in covenant. Now, while David's rule was confined to the geographic limits of Israel, when one explores the language used to describe the reign of Solomon, he sees typological signposts pointing to the future global extension of the reign of God's vicegerent.

As King David prepares to anoint his son, Solomon, as the new king of Israel, one sees protologically evocative language, especially that associated with the dominion

---

[50]G. K. Beale, *The Temple and the Church's Mission: A Biblical Theology of the Dwelling Place of God*, NSBT (Downers Grove: Inter Varsity, 2004), pp. 107-08.

mandate of Genesis 1:28: 'Yours, O LORD, is the greatness and the power and the glory and the victory and the majesty, for all that is in the *heavens and in the earth* is yours. Yours is the *kingdom* [הַמַּמְלָכָה (hammamlākāʰ), or dominion], O LORD, and you are exalted as head above all. Both riches and honor come from you, and *you rule over all*' (1 Chron. 29:11-12; emphasis). In David's statement one finds the protological elements of the heavens and earth, dominion, and rule over the creation. Beale explains that 'David uses language synonymous to that of Genesis 1:28 to praise God himself because he is the one who "makes great and strengthens" his human vice-regents to rule under his hand.'[51] When Solomon finally builds the temple, one sees a picture of a king who offers sacrifices and has international influence, a typological portrait that the Son of the ruler of heaven and earth will one day build an eschatological dwelling place for God, one that will extend throughout the earth (1 Kings 5–10; 2 Chron. 1–9). One finds further confirmation of the global extent of the reign of the heir of David in Psalm 110.

In Psalm 110 David famously writes of the eschatological priest-king, 'The LORD says to my Lord: "Sit at my right hand, until I make your enemies your footstool" ' (v. 1). One should note that in addition to David's kingly and priestly activity, as noted above, one sees prophetic activity in his authorship of Scripture. Nevertheless, concerning this verse and Christ's use of it (Luke 20:41-44), Vos explains that

> the Messiah must be God's Son in order to be capable of the things predicated of Him in the Psalm. Here, then, the divine sonship of Jesus is represented as the basis of that higher character of the Messiahship which expressed His own ideal: because He is the Son of God, He rules the world to come. Nor do we think it straining the words too much if we find in Jesus' statement the

---

[51]Beale, *The Temple*, p. 108.

implication that the Messianic sovereignty must cover the world to come because only as an inhabitant of the world to come could David be subject to it.[52]

Vos is correct to note that the priest-king will rule over the world, something that has been hinted at from the very beginning, from Genesis 1:28. Tying the rule of the first Adam, God's vicegerent, to the rule of this future priest-king that will reign over the nations, Hans-Joachim Kraus interestingly notes that 'in the period of the kings Yahweh's wars are waged by the king; they act as "viceroys of Yahweh" and representatives of his royal power, and God acts through them.'[53] One finds, then, that the Davidic covenant is rooted, not only in God's covenants with the patriarchs and Israel but ultimately the trajectories of protology – here in shadows and types one sees that a great prophet-priest-king will build a dwelling place for God and rule over the earth as his vicegerent. This eschatological vicegerent will be faithful and obedient to the will of his Father, unlike the first disobedient vicegerent.

Summary
The patterns of protology are repeated throughout redemptive history. In many treatments of the doctrine of creation in contemporary dogmatics, creation drifts into distant memory and is often not interrelated with the other loci of systematic theology. But it must be recognized that other doctrinal loci are informed, and even hinge, upon a correct understanding of the beginning. This is certainly evident in the protological elements and themes repeated throughout the Old Testament and especially in the Noahic, Abrahamic,

---

[52]Geerhardus Vos, *The Self-Disclosure of Jesus: The Modern Debate about the Messianic Consciousness*, ed., J. G. Vos (1926; 1953; Phillipsburg: P & R, 1978), pp. 165-66.

[53]Hans-Joachim Kraus, *Psalms 60-150*, trans. Hilton C. Oswald (Minneapolis: Fortress, 1989), p. 349.

Mosaic and Davidic covenants. In tracing out the patterns of protology in these covenants, one does not want to bypass an important point, namely, the theological underpinning of the progress of redemptive history. The theological relationship between the covenant of works and the Noahic, Abrahamic, and Mosaic covenants must be explored before one can proceed to examine the work of the second Adam.

The theological foundation: the covenant of grace

Before proceeding to an examination of the work of the second Adam, it is important that one examine the theological foundation for the covenants subsequent to the fall. A quick reading of the covenants might lead one to the conclusion that with each successive covenant head, Noah, Abraham, and Moses, there is a theological reincarnation of Adam, each being been given the same task as his predecessor. The impression might be that, with each covenantal administration of the patterns of protology, the task of spreading the image of God and temple throughout the earth, and ruling as God's vicegerent, is given to Noah, Abraham, and Moses as if they, or those under their authority, can carry out the work of the first Adam. Such a conclusion fails to take several important factors into consideration.

First, one must recall that on the heels of the failed work of the first Adam, God himself promised victory over the serpent and the deleterious effects of Adam's rebellion (Gen. 3:15). What was Adam's response to God's promise? Adam renamed his wife, which is significant. After the pronouncement of the divine curses upon the man and woman, Adam named his wife a second time. Adam first named his wife, 'woman' (Gen. 2:23), but after the fall named her חַוָּה (ḥawwāʰ) or, 'Eve,' which means, 'giver of life.' The LXX renders the woman's name as, Ζωή (zōē) or 'life.' It is likely that this event is a declaration of faith on the part of Adam; he has faith that God will bring about the promised redemption through the seed of the woman. Accordingly, Adam names his wife, 'giver of life,' and the subsequent comment from the narrator therefore explains that 'she was the mother of all living'.[54] As H. C. Leupold comments,

> by the significant nature of the name employed, as well as by the significant way in which the matter is reported at this important juncture, we are to understand that Adam refers to the things implied in the promise of victory over the devil. In other words, he here gives evidence not only of believing that God spoke the truth but evidence of belief in the salvation which God had promised. This, then, was on Adam's part, as far as was possible under the circumstances, a true and living faith in Christ.

It is important to note, however, with Leupold that 'this faith of his surely could not have all the clearness that marks the faith of New Testament believers.'[55] What this implies, then, is that by virtue of the fact that Adam gave his wife the name of 'Eve', it means that Adam repented from his sin and placed his faith in the promised seed of the woman to deliver them both from sin, death, and the serpent. Through Eve the promised deliverer would conquer the serpent and reverse the disastrous

---

[54]Martin Luther, *Lectures on Genesis*, LW, vol. 1, ed. Jaroslav Pelikan (St. Louis: Concordia, 1958), p. 220; Kidner, *Genesis*, p. 72; Morris, *Genesis*, p. 129; von Rad, *Genesis*, p. 96. Once again, Morris makes questionable typological interpretations on this verse when he states that 'Eve has become a type of our heavenly home;' he cites Galatians 4.26 (*Genesis*, p. 129). Calvin argues that when Adam gives his wife the name of *Eve*, he is simply celebrating the fact that God has not immediately brought death upon them (*Genesis*, CTS [1847; Grand Rapids: Baker, 1993], p. 181). Contra Sarna (*Genesis*, p. 29) and Umberto Cassuto (*Commentary on the Book of Genesis*, Part One, *From Adam to Noah*, trans. Israel Abrahams [Jerusalem: Magnes Press, 1998], pp. 170-71), who believe that there is a word-play between חַוָּה (ḥawwāʰ) and the Aramaic word חִיוְיָא (ḥywyʾ) or 'serpent' (cf. Wenham, *Genesis*, p. 84; Leupold, *Genesis*, p. 178; von Rad, *Genesis*, p. 96). According to this view, Adam gives his wife a name that will remind her of her sin with the serpent.

[55]Leupold, *Genesis*, p. 177.

consequences of Adam's sin. In other words, Adam recognized that the seed of the woman would have to carry out his failed work.

Second, incidental attention has been drawn to the differences between the covenant of works and the subsequent covenants with Noah, Abraham, and Moses. In the covenant with Noah, God appropriated the rainbow as a sign of his covenant with Noah and all creation that he will not destroy the earth by means of a flood (Gen. 9:11-16). In other words, God grants a 'stay of execution', of sorts, upon the creation; he would not visit the creation with his wrath in this manner again. This is, of course, the grace of God, both common and special. Common grace falls upon the creation and those outside of God's electing love, and special grace falls upon those in covenant with him. This means that the renewed administration of the dominion mandate has a foundation of grace rather than being based on merit, as in the pre-fall covenant with Adam. Approaching the covenant with Abraham, the same emphasis upon grace re-emerges. It is significant that Adam received the dominion mandate as command: 'Be fruitful and multiply and fill the earth and subdue it' (Gen. 1:28), whereas God gave Abraham a promise: 'I will make of you a great nation, and I will bless you and make your name great, so that you will be a blessing' (Gen. 12:2).[56] The goal of the covenant of works is still before Abraham, but the means of attainment has changed; it is no longer Adam, or man, but God himself, who will bring about the intended results. The same holds true for the covenant made with Israel. Though Israel is God's son, placed in a paradise, and given the mandate to be a light unto the nations unto the ends of the earth, just as Adam who was God's son before them, Israel was constantly reminded that it was God who was ultimately at work in them. God was the one who delivered them

---

[56]Wright, *People of God*, p. 263.

from bondage (Exod. 20:1); he was the source of their sanctification (Exod. 33:13).

Third, there is a great difference between the priestly activity of the first Adam and that of subsequent covenants with Noah, Abraham, and Israel. When Noah, Abraham, and the patriarchs constructed their altars, miniature temples, or places where they met and worshiped God, they offered blood sacrifices. In the garden-temple Adam may have offered sacrifices, either grain or thank-offerings, but these were in celebration of God's abundant blessings, not due to the presence of sin. After the fall blood sacrifices were required to approach God – something adumbrated in Adam and Eve's post-fall vestments, elucidated in the sacrifices of Abel, Noah, Abraham, and the patriarchs, and further revealed in greater detail in the covenant with Israel (e.g. Exod. 29:1ff.; Lev. 16:1ff.). Recall that after the fall, Adam's approach to God was barred by cherubim with flaming swords (Gen. 3:24), a reality represented by the embroidered cherubim adorning the veil that barred access to the holy of holies, God's throne room. After the fall, man cannot accomplish the work of the first Adam. He can neither extract himself from his fallen condition, nor can he enter into God's presence apart from God's appointed means. These factors render important the theological foundation of God's post-fall dealings with man, namely, the covenant of grace.

God's gracious dealings with fallen man begin with the *protoevangelium* of Genesis 3:15 and culminate in the work of the second Adam. This same *evangelium*, or gospel, undergirded the covenant with Noah and was given to Abraham: 'And the Scripture, foreseeing that God would justify the Gentiles by faith, preached the gospel beforehand to Abraham, saying, "In you shall all the nations be blessed" ' (Gal. 3:8; cf. Gen. 12:3; 18:18; 28:14).[57] Israel's covenant is based upon the same gospel promise that was given to Abraham (Exod. 3:15; 6:3-8), a promise that is ultimately fulfilled in the person and work of the second Adam, Jesus Christ.[58] Theologians have historically labeled this administration of God's promise of redemption as the *covenant of grace*. The Westminster Confession provides a helpful definition of the covenant of grace: 'Man, by his fall, having made himself incapable of life by that covenant, the Lord was pleased to make a second, commonly called the Covenant of Grace, whereby He freely offers unto sinners life and salvation by Jesus Christ, requiring of them faith in Him, that they may be saved; and promising to give unto all those that are ordained unto eternal life His Holy Spirit, to make them willing, and able to believe' (WCF 7.3).[59] Though there are various ways in which the covenant of grace is administered, visible in the differences between the Noahic, Abrahamic, and Mosaic covenants, at its core lies the same promise of Genesis 3:15 – the same gospel.

In order to understand the relationship between the covenant of works, the covenant of grace, and the Noahic, Abrahamic, and Mosaic covenants, one must recognize two things. First, at the level of the *ordo salutis*, all people after the fall are saved in the same manner – by faith in Christ, a reality set forth in Genesis 3:15 and its subsequent republications with greater clarity and specificity. In this regard the Noahic, Abrahamic, and Mosaic covenants fall under the rubric of the covenant of grace – the outworking of the *protoevangelium*. Second, on the level of the *historia salutis* Noah, Abraham, and Israel are shadows, or types, of the second Adam who is to come. Again, it is helpful to remember the interpretive relationship between the Old Testament and New Testament. The Westminster divines explain

---

[57]So James D. G. Dunn, *The Epistle to the Galatians*, BNTC (Peabody: Hendrickson, 1993), p. 166; cf. F. F. Bruce, *The Epistle to the Galatians*, NIGTC (1982; Grand Rapids: Eerdmans, 1992), pp. 156-57.

[58]Contra Ryrie, *Dispensationalism*, pp. 61-62, 126, 131, 132-55.

[59]Cf. Louis Berkhof, *Systematic Theology* (1932, 38; Grand Rapids: Eerdmans, 1996), p. 277.

the relationship of the *ordo* and *historia salutis* as it is bound up in the covenant of grace:

Q. How was the covenant of grace administered under the Old Testament?

A. The covenant of grace was administered under the Old Testament, by promises, prophecies, sacrifices, circumcision, the passover, and other types and ordinances, which did fore-signify Christ then to come, and were for that time sufficient to build up the elect in faith in the promised Messiah, by whom they then had full remission of sin, and eternal salvation (*Larger Catechism 34*).

The Old Testament foresignifies Christ, the second Adam, in shadows and types, though all of God's people, both Old Testament and New Testament, are saved by faith in the promised Messiah. Some might think that the Old Testament types look back to Adam in the covenant of works in some sense. While it is true that there are connections to Adam and protology in Noah, Abraham, and Israel, one must recognize that Noah, Abraham, and Israel do not look backward but ultimately point forward. Indeed, Adam, Noah, Abraham, and Israel are forward-looking shadows of Christ, the second Adam.

Conclusion

The three major covenants leading up to the ministry of Christ have been surveyed. In each of these covenants the themes and patterns of protology do not drift away but stand clearly in the foreground. The same themes of spreading the image of God and worship within a covenantal context are repeated in the Noahic, Abrahamic, and Mosaic covenants. These covenants are not distinct and separate attempts to re-establish the broken covenant of works, but are the outworking of the one gospel promise of Genesis 3:15. The covenants all in some way hearken back to the creation and the work of the first Adam but ultimately serve as shadows and types of the second Adam. It is the work of the second Adam that must now be explored.

5

The Work of the Second Adam

Introduction

Having surveyed the scope of pre-redemptive and redemptive history beginning with the work of the first Adam, the investigation has determined that the first Adam was essentially the first prophet, priest, and king. The work of the first Adam was established within the context of a covenantal relationship. Within that covenantal relationship, Adam was to spread the image of God to the ends of the earth, extend the temple to the ends of the earth, exercise dominion over the creation, and accomplish these tasks with the assistance of his helpmate. The study has also surveyed the three major covenants in the Old Testament: the Noahic, Abrahamic, and Mosaic, to demonstrate that the goals of the adamic covenant of works were republished in the subsequent covenants. These three covenants, couched in the imagery of protology, point forward to the person and work of the second Adam. One must now explore the connections between protology and christology. First, this chapter will explore the similarities between the two Adams.[1] Second, it will look at the life, death, and

---

[1]For a brief summary of the similarities between the first and second Adams, see Karl Barth, *Church Dogmatics*, 3.1, trans. J. W. Edwards, et al. (1958; Edinburgh: T & T Clark, 1998), p. 204.

resurrection of Christ to see the connections between protology and christology. Third, it will show how protology, christology, and ecclesiology relate, namely, that the Church is the helpmate of the second Adam. Fourth, the chapter will explore how the second Adam fulfills the dominion mandate. Fifth, and last, it will examine the completed work of the second Adam. One may therefore proceed to the first section, the similarities between the two Adams.

Similarities between the two Adams

As the initial chapter on the image of God intimated, there are several important similarities between the first and second Adams: image, sonship, and the *munus triplex*, or threefold office.

Image of God

Genesis states that Adam was created in God's image, though one should not forget that man, male and female, comprise the image (Gen. 1:26-27). Nevertheless, Christ, as the second Adam, is not created in the image of God but rather is the image of God. This is attested in more than one place in the New Testament: 'Christ, who is the image of God' (2 Cor. 4:4); and 'He is the image of the invisible God' (Col. 1:15). This is the first significant parallel between Adam and Christ. There is a second, namely, the sonship of Adam and Christ.

God's Son

Adam is called God's son (Luke 3:38). Adam's sonship is also implied by the normal relationship between father and son – the son bears the father's image. This connection emerges in Adam's relationship to his sons. Note how the author begins Genesis 5 with a restatement of the creation of Adam in God's image: 'When God created man, he made him in the likeness of God' (Gen. 5:1). Subsequent to this statement, the author describes the birth of Seth with the same language:

'When Adam had lived 130 years, he fathered a son in his own likeness, after his image, and named him Seth' (Gen. 5:3), lending credence to the concept that Adam was God's son. The son-image-bearing connection is further amplified in how the author of Hebrews begins his epistle, writing that God 'has in these last days spoken to us by his Son, whom he has appointed heir of all things, through whom also he made the worlds; who being the brightness of his glory and the express image of his person' (Heb. 1:2-3; NKJV). Here the ideas of image-bearing and sonship are inextricably intertwined.[2] This brings the second major similarity between the first and second Adams to the forefront.

The threefold office

One of the things made clear throughout the study thus far is the nature of the work of the first Adam. Given the dominion mandate (Gen. 1:28), it is plain that Adam was God's vicegerent to rule the earth. Adam was therefore a king. Given the combination of the verbs 'to work and keep' (Gen. 2:15) in connection with Adam's garden-temple responsibilities, he was given priestly, not agricultural responsibilities (cf. Num. 3:7-8; 4:23-24, 26). Adam was therefore a priest. Adam's responsibilities included spreading the image of God and his garden-temple to the ends of the earth. In addition to procreation, this would have ostensibly been supplemented through preaching.[3] Adam therefore had a prophetic aspect to his responsibilities and work, meaning that Adam held the same *munus triplex* that Christ holds: prophet, priest, and king. In this regard Louis Berkhof writes that

---

[2] William L. Lane, *Hebrews 9-13*, WBC, vol. 47b (Dallas: Word, 1991), pp. 12-13; also see Paul Ellingworth, *The Epistle to the Hebrews*, NIGTC (Grand Rapids: Eerdmans, 1993), p. 99.

[3] See e.g. Martin Luther, *Lectures on Genesis*, LW, vol. 1, ed. Jaroslav Pelikan (St. Louis: Concordia, 1958), p. 80.

the fact that Christ was anointed to a threefold office finds its explanation in the fact that man was originally intended for this threefold office and work. As created by God, he was prophet, priest, and king, and as such was endowed with knowledge and understanding, with righteousness and holiness, and with dominion over the lower creation.[4]

These three offices do not arise *de novo* in the ministry of Christ but have their roots in protology. Berkhof goes on to note that Christ as prophet 'represents God with man; as Priest He represents man in the presence of God, and as King He exercises dominion and restores the original dominion of man.'[5] These roles – as God's image-bearers, Adam and Christ as God's sons, and as possessors of the threefold office – must be kept in mind as one continues to explore the work of the second Adam. What about the threefold work of Christ, his life, death, and resurrection and its connections to protology?

The life of Christ

Luke 4:1-14: the temptation of Christ
One of the major themes of protology, indeed of the whole of Scripture, is the failed probation of the first Adam. Adam as the prophet, priest, and king of the garden-temple was expected to obey God's command and guard the temple from anything that was unclean. Adam instead obeyed his helpmate, disobeyed the command of God, and failed to guard the temple from the serpent (Gen. 2:16-17; 3:6-7). With the ministry of Christ, one of the first events recounted in the pages of the Gospels is Jesus' temptation in the wilderness. Perhaps what

---

[4]Louis Berkhof, *Systematic Theology: New Combined Edition* (1932, 38; Grand Rapids: Eerdmans, 1996), p. 357; also W. J. Dumbrell, *Covenant and Creation: A Theology of the Old Testament Covenants* (1984; Carlisle: Paternoster, 2002), p. 45.

[5]Berkhof, *Systematic Theology*, p. 357.

many do not notice, however, is the connection between the probation of Adam and Christ's temptation in the wilderness. It is important to take note that Luke gives the genealogy of Christ, which traces the lineage of Christ to Adam, the son of God (Luke 3:38). Immediately subsequent to listing the name of Adam, Luke describes the temptation of Christ in the wilderness. As Earle Ellis comments, 'Jesus not only is the heir of David and seed of Abraham (Matt. 1:1); he also is the second or "eschatological" Adam and the "son of God".'[6] Christ, as the second Adam, takes up the work of the first Adam. Therefore, at the beginning of his public ministry Christ undergoes temptation, just as the first Adam was tempted.[7] In fact, scholars argue that the first and second Adam parallel governs the structure of Luke's Gospel at this point.[8] There are yet further similarities between protology and christology.

Christ, unlike Adam, rebuffed the temptations of the serpent, who is now explicitly identified as the devil (Luke 4:2). Just as he did in the garden the serpent, Satan, tempts the second Adam with the promise of God-like qualities, namely, authority over the nations – the reign of a king (Luke 4:6-7). Satan, once again, speaks in half-truths, as the nations are not under his absolute authority (cf. 4:31-37; 8:26-39; Matt. 4:10). While Satan does wield great influence over the nations, his offer has been characterized as an 'oversell'.[9] More important, however, are the stark contrasts between Adam and Christ. Adam had an abundance of food (Gen. 2:16); Christ had been fasting for forty days (Luke 4:2). Adam dwelled in the garden-temple, paradise; Christ, on the

---

[6]E. Earle Ellis, *The Gospel of Luke*, NCBC (1966; Grand Rapids: Eerdmans, 1996), p. 93.

[7]William Hendriksen, *Luke*, NTC (Grand Rapids: Baker, 1978), p. 230.

[8]Darrell L. Bock, *Luke 1–9.50*, BECNT (Grand Rapids: Baker, 1994), pp. 348-49.

[9]Bock, *Luke*, p. 376.

other hand, underwent his probation in the barren wilderness (Luke 4:1). And unlike Adam, Christ was perfectly obedient to the will of his heavenly Father.[10]

Beyond these immediate connections to the first Adam, there are also further connections to protology surrounding the probation of Christ. Recall that the creation emerged from the primeval waters on day three (Gen. 1:9); the creation subsequent to the flood emerged from the waters once again (Gen. 8:13); similarly, Israel, God's son, as a nation, was born from the waters of the Red Sea (Exod. 15:19). In each of these instances, not only does the creation and God's representative emerge from the waters, but so too the Holy Spirit, or a representation thereof, is also present: the Holy Spirit hovering over the primeval waters like a bird (Gen. 1:2); the dove hovering over the receding flood waters (Gen. 8:14); and the pillar of cloud that accompanied the Israelites through the Red Sea hovering like a bird (Deut. 32:11; Exod. 13:21-22; cf. Hag. 2:5; Isa. 63:11). These events, which have their roots in protology, are repeated in various forms in subsequent redemptive history and serve as types that find their fulfillment in Christ.

In this connection Geerhardus Vos acknowledges that while the Old Testament does not compare the Holy Spirit to a dove, the Spirit does have avian-like features in his activity in Genesis 1. Vos writes regarding the baptism of Christ and the presence of the Holy Spirit that

> the Old Testament nowhere compares the Spirit to a dove. It does represent the Spirit as hovering, brooding over the waters of chaos, in order to produce life out of the primeval matter. This might be found suggestive of the thought, that the work of the Messiah constituted a second creation, bound together with the first through this function of the Spirit in connection with it.[11]

---

[10]Hendriksen, *Luke*, pp. 233-34.

What Vos has stated somewhat tentatively one can state with a greater degree of certainty given the results of the investigation thus far. The first creation, and with it the first Adam, emerged from the waters by the superintendence of the Holy Spirit. Subsequent to Adam's fall, this theme is repeated with Noah and Israel, types that point to the second Adam and the new heavens and earth. With Christ's baptism a new creation once again emerges from the water, superintended by the Holy Spirit (Luke 3:31-32). Under the ministry of the second Adam, the new creation emerges from the waters of baptism. This connection between the waters of baptism and the new creation is confirmed elsewhere in the New Testament.

The themes of protology resurface in conjunction with soteriology and eschatology, especially as it relates to the flood and baptism. In 1 Peter, the apostle explains that Noah and his family 'were saved through water' (1 Pet. 3:20). One must not forget that the waters of the deluge do not arise out of thin air but are connected with the waters of creation – the waters above the firmament that lie before the throne of God and the waters of the deep (cf. Gen. 1:2, 6-8; Rev. 4:6). When God unleashed the flood waters, he released the waters that were originally restrained at the creation, 'deep ... waters' and the 'windows of the heavens' (cf. Gen. 1:2, 6-8; 7:11). In other words, when God brought the deluge it was an undoing of the creation.[12] It did not simply rain – the flood

---

[11]Geerhardus Vos, *Biblical Theology* (1948; Edinburgh: Banner of Truth, 1996), p. 322.

[12]So Nahum Sarna, *Genesis*, JPSTC (Philadelphia: JPS, 1989), p. 55; Herman Gunkel, *Genesis*, trans. Mark E. Biddle (Macon: Mercer UP, 1997), pp. 145-46; Derek Kidner, *Genesis*, TOTC (Downers Grove: InterVarsity, 1967), pp. 90-91; Gerhard von Rad, *Genesis*, OTL (Philadelphia: Westminster, 1972), p. 128; Gordon J. Wenham, *Genesis 1-15*, WBC, vol. 1 (Dallas: Word, 1987), p. 181; similarly Claus Westermann, *Genesis 1-11*, trans. John J. Scullion (Minneapolis: Fortress, 1994), pp. 433-34; H. C. Leupold makes the connection between the waters of the deep in Genesis 1:2 but denies

was both a natural and supernatural event. When God re-created the earth, the waters of the flood were parallel to the waters of Genesis 1:2.[13] In other words, the flood waters are the waters of (re)creation. In the flood God returned the earth to its chaotic state of Genesis 1:2. The connection between the deluge and new creation carries over to the significance of the waters of baptism; baptism is the water of (re)creation. Peter identifies the flood waters by which Noah and his family were saved as the type; he identifies the waters of baptism as the antitype: 'There is also an antitype which now saves us – baptism ... through the resurrection of Jesus Christ' (1 Pet. 3:21-22, NKJV; cf. 1 Cor. 10:1ff).[14] Peter connects baptism to the deluge, that is, the waters of (re)creation. Though this connection will be explored in greater detail, one should not miss the apostle's point, that baptism is connected to the work of the second Adam, to Christ.[15] The following chart illustrates that there is an intimate connection between the protological elements of water, the presence of the Holy Spirit, God's son, and Christ's baptism as the second Adam.

There is yet another passage that deals with the probation of the second Adam.

---

the connection between Genesis 1:7 and Revelation 4:6 (*Exposition of Genesis*, vol. 1 [Grand Rapids: Baker, 1942], p. 296); contra Henry Morris who writes about the waters above the firmament which 'constituted the vast vaporous canopy which maintained the earth as a beautiful greenhouse, preventing cold temperatures and therefore preventing wind and rain storms. Being in the vapor state, it was invisible and fully transparent, but nevertheless contained vast quantities of water extending far out into space' (*The Genesis Record: A Scientific & Devotional Commentary on the Book of Beginnings* [Grand Rapids: Baker, 1976], p. 194).

[13]Warren Austin Gage, *The Gospel of Genesis* (1984; Eugene: Wipf & Stock, 2001), pp. 10-11.

[14]Leonhard Goppelt, *Typos* (Grand Rapids: Eerdmans, 1982), pp. 155-57; cf. J. Ramsey Michaels, *1 Peter*, WBC (Dallas: Word, 1988), p. 214.

[15]Vos, *Biblical Theology*, p. 145.

Element	Gen. 1–3 First Adam	Flood / Type	Exodus / Type	Second Adam /Antitype
Water	'Darkness was over the face of the deep' (Gen. 1:2b).	'The waters prevailed on the earth' (Gen. 7:24).	'The LORD drove the sea back by a strong east wind [rûªḥ]' (Exod.14:21).	'Jesus was baptized, immediately he went up from the water' (Matt. 3:16a).
Spirit	'The Spirit [rûªḥ] of God was hovering' (Gen. 1:2c).	'God made a wind [rûªḥ] blow over the earth, and the waters sub-sided' (Gen. 8:1). 'Then he sent forth a dove from him, to see if the waters had subsided from the face of the ground' (Gen. 8:8).	'He found [Israel] in a desert land ... As an eagle stirs up its nest, hovers over its young' (Deut. 32:10-11). 'Then he remembered ... Moses and his people. Where is he who brought them up out of the sea ... who put in the midst of them his Holy Spirit' (Isa. 63:11).	'The heavens were opened to him, and he saw the Spirit of God descending like a dove' (Matt. 3:16b).
God's son	'God created man in his own image' (Gen. 1:27).	'Noah was a righteous man, blameless in his generation. Noah walked with God' (Gen. 6:9).	'Israel is my firstborn son' (Exod. 4:22).	'This is my beloved Son, with whom I am well pleased' (Matt. 3:17).
Baptism	Cf. Gen. 1:2; Gen. 7:24; 1 Pet. 3:20-21a.	In the days of Noah ... eight souls, were saved through water. There is also an anti-type which now saves us – baptism' (1 Pet. 3:20-21a).	'All passed through the sea, and all were baptized into Moses in the cloud and in the sea' (1 Cor. 10:1-2).	Matt. 3:16a.

Philippians 2:5-11: A hymn to the second Adam
Chapter 2 of Philippians is one with which many are
familiar but nonetheless fail to recognize its connections
to protology. Paul begins this pericope with the
exhortation to the Philippians that they need to have
the mind of Christ (v. 5). Then in verse 6a Paul explains
that Christ was 'in the form of God,' ἐν μορφῇ θεοῦ (en
morphē theou). What, however, does it mean to be in the
form of God? Though there are various explanations of
this phrase, the best takes this phrase to indicate the
'form which truly and fully expresses the being which
underlies it'. Peter O'Brien explains that

> the expression does not refer simply to external
> appearance but pictures the preexistent Christ as
> clothed in the garments of divine majesty and splendour.
> He was in the form of God, sharing God's glory. ἐν μορφῇ
> θεοῦ thus corresponds with Jn. 17:5 ('the glory I had
> with you before the world began') and reminds one of
> Heb. 1:3 ('the radiance of God's glory and the exact
> representation of his being').[16]

A picture of this glory appears in the temple vision
of Isaiah – the prophet sees a christophany, not a
theophany (cf. Isa. 6:1-8; John 12:41). That Christ is
ἐν μορφῇ θεοῦ (en morphē theou) has important protological
connections.

Though there is disagreement among scholars, a case
can be made that Paul's usage of 'form' or μορφη, (morphē)
is connected to Genesis 1:26-27. Herman Ridderbos
argues that Paul's usage of μορφη, (morphē) is parallel to
the phrase 'image of God,' εἰκὼν τοῦ θεοῦ (eikôn tou theou)
(2 Cor. 4:4; Col. 1:15). Ridderbos also draws attention
to Paul's synonymous use of the terms μορφη, (morphē)
and εἰκών (eikôn): 'Thus it is said in 2 Cor. 3:18 that we
shall be trans*formed* (μεταμορφούμεθα) [metamorphoumetha]

---

[16]Peter T. O'Brien, *The Epistle to the Philippians*, NIGTC (Grand
Rapids: Eedrmans, 1991), pp. 210-11.

after the same *image* (εἰκόνα) [eikôna], namely, of Christ' (Rom. 8:29; Phil. 3:21; Gal. 4:19; 1 Cor. 15:45, 49). This means, therefore, that verse 6a has important connections to Genesis 1:26-27.[17] Commenting on a web of Pauline passages and their connection to Genesis 1:27 (cf. 2 Cor. 4:4; Col. 1:15; 1 Cor. 11:7; Rom. 1:23; 3:23; 8:29ff; 2 Cor. 3:18; Phil. 2:6) Ridderbos writes that 'we can come to no other conclusion, therefore, than that in the above mentioned passages Paul has denoted the divine glory of Christ both in his pre-existence and in his exaltation with a qualification that also held for the first Adam, although, of course, in another sense appropriate to the first Adam.'[18] The connection of verse 2:6a to Genesis 1:26-27 has further implications when verse 6b-c is examined.

In verse 6b-c, Paul writes that Christ 'did not count equality with God a thing to be grasped' ὑπάρχων οὐχ ἁρπαγμὸν ἡγήσατο τὸ εἶναι ἴσα θεῷ (*uparchôn ouch harpagmon egêsato to einai isa theô*). If one goes to verse 6c first, he sees that Paul presents the idea of equality with God. Given the overall trajectory of verse 6, namely that it rests upon Genesis 1:26-27, equality with God hearkens back to the temptation of the first Adam: 'You will be like God' (Gen. 3:5). This helps one understand the import of verse 6b: Christ 'did not consider equality with God a thing to be grasped.' The Greek term behind the word 'grasped' is ἁρπαγμός (*harpagmos*) which is derived from ἁρπαζω (*harpadzo*) and literally means 'to snatch' or 'seize' and denotes 'the act of snatching or seizing.' Within the context of Philippians 2:6 as a

---

[17]Herman Ridderbos, *Paul: An Outline of His Theology*, trans. John Richard de Witt (1975; Grand Rapids: Eerdmans, 1997), p. 74; also John G. Gibbs, 'The Relation Between Creation and Redemption According to Phil. 2.5-11,' *NT* 12 (1970), pp. 274-75; Seyoon Kim, *Paul and the New Perspective* (Grand Rapids: Eerdmans, 2002), p. 173; cf. O'Brien, *Philippians*, pp. 263-68; C. K. Barrett, *From First Adam to Last* (London: Adam & Charles Black, 1962), p. 71.

[18]Ridderbos, *Paul*, p. 72.

whole, however, it is part of an idiomatic expression to convey the idea that Christ did not use his equality with God to his own advantage.[19] The Adam and Christ parallel emerges, then, when one considers that Adam attempted to grasp equality with God, whereas the second Adam did not use his equality with God to his own advantage. The second Adam succeeded where the first Adam failed. Adam tried to grasp equality with God by eating from the fruit of the tree from which he was prohibited. In contradistinction, Christ took the form of sinful man and was obedient to the will of his heavenly Father throughout the entirety of his life, even unto death, death on a cross (Phil. 2:8-9).[20]

Clearly, the life of the second Adam is rooted in protology – the failed work of the first Adam.[21] The first Adam failed in his probation in the garden, but the second Adam was perfectly obedient to the will of his heavenly Father in his own probation in the wilderness and beyond. Oscar Cullmann summarizes well the connections between Philippians 2:5-11 and Genesis 1–3 when he writes:

All the statements of Phil. 2:6ff. are to be understood from the standpoint of the Old Testament history of Adam. Adam was created in the image of God, but he lost that image because he wanted to grasp equality with God. Unlike Adam, the Heavenly Man, who in his pre-existence represented the true image of God, humbled himself in obedience and now receives the equality with God he did not grasp as a 'robbery.'[22]

---

[19]O'Brien, *Philippians*, pp. 212, 215; Ridderbos, *Paul*, pp. 74-75; Gibbs, 'Creation and Redemption,' p. 277.

[20]Thomas R. Schreiner, *Paul Apostle of God's Glory in Christ* (Downers Grove: InterVarsity Press, 2001), p. 172.

[21]Gibbs, 'Creation and Redemption,' pp. 280-81.

[22]Oscar Cullmann, *The Christology of the New Testament*, trans. Shirley C. Guthrie and Charles A. M. Hall (Philadelphia: Westminster, 1963), p. 181.

The work of the second Adam, however, does not end in his life. Rather, as in Philippians 2:8-9, it proceeds to the cross.

The death of Christ

Romans 5:12-19: Imputation of the work of the first and second Adams

A major emphasis in the work of the second Adam, of course, is his obedience unto death on the cross – his substitutionary atonement on behalf of the elect – the penalty for the broken covenant of works as well as for actual sin they have personally committed. Nowhere else does the relationship between the work of the first and second Adams, or protology and christology, become evident as it does in Romans 5:12-19. This passage has already been explored in connection with the covenant of works, so that exegetical data need not be revisited. One should nevertheless not bypass the crux of this passage in its connection with the work of the second Adam: 'For as by the one man's disobedience the many were made sinners, so by the one man's obedience the many will be made righteous' (Rom. 5:19). It is essential that the connections between the work of the first and second Adams are recognized. The work of each Adam is applied to those who are represented by each, by the imputation of sin and righteousness.

As previously noted, Adam was the covenantal head of mankind. Upon his failed probation, the guilt of his sin was imputed to his progeny. This is stated quite clearly in Romans 5:12: 'Therefore, just as sin came into the world through one man, and death through sin, and so death spread to all men because all sinned.' One must note the connection between the sin of 'one man' and its result that 'all sinned'. Paul speaks elsewhere to this matter when he says that 'in Adam all die' (1 Cor. 15:22a).[23] John Murray observes that 'the parallel to the imputation of Adam's sin is the imputation of Christ's righteousness. Or, to use Paul's own terms, being "constituted sinners" through the disobedience of Adam is parallel to being "constituted righteous" through the obedience of Christ.'[24] Paul draws this out, for example, when he writes concerning the faith of Abraham and its relationship to the work of Christ: 'And he received the sign of circumcision, a seal of the righteousness of the faith which he had while still uncircumcised, that he might be the father of all those who believe, though they are uncircumcised, that righteousness might be imputed to them also' (Rom. 4:11, NKJV) and, 'Now it was not written for his sake alone that it was imputed to him, but also for us. It shall be imputed to us who believe in him who raised up Jesus our Lord from the dead' (Rom. 4:23-24, NKJV).[25] Christ imputes his righteousness to his people and in turn the sin of the elect is imputed to Christ (2 Cor. 5:21). This aspect of imputation, namely the bearing of the guilt of the sin of the first Adam as well as the personal sins of the elect, emerges quite clearly in

---

[23]John Murray, *The Imputation of Adam's Sin* (Phillipsburg: P & R, 1959), pp. 68-69, esp. pp. 71-95; contra Wright who argues in connection with Romans 5:12 that it is not necessary to espouse 'any particular theory of the mode by which sin is transmitted' (N. T. Wright, *Romans*, NIB [Nashville: Abingdon, 2002], p. 526).

[24]Murray, *Imputation*, p. 76.

[25]Contra Wright who defines the righteousness of Romans 4:11, not as the righteousness of Christ which is imputed by God to the believer, but as 'covenant membership'. Wright is also silent regarding the significance of imputation in Romans 4:23-24 (*Romans*, pp. 494, 501-02). Also contra Dunn who argues that these passages, esp. Romans 4:23-24, refer to future justification (James D. G. Dunn, *Romans*, WBC, vol. 38a [Dallas: Word, 1988], p. 223). Cf. C. E. B. Cranfield, *Romans*, vol. 1, ICC (1975; Edinburgh: T & T Clark, 2001), pp. 236, 250; Thomas Schreiner, *Romans*, BECNT (Grand Rapids: Baker, 1998), pp. 224, 242; Douglas Moo, *Romans*, NICNT (Grand Rapids: Eerdmans, 1991), p. 295; J. V. Fesko, 'A Critical Examination of N. T. Wright's Doctrine of Justification,' *The Confessional Presbyterian* 1 (2005), pp. 102-16, esp. pp. 106-12.

the Abrahamic covenant and its subsequent New Testament interpretation.

Old Testament background: the Abrahamic covenant
In the Abrahamic covenant the mysterious events of the evening unfold subsequent to God giving Abraham his covenant promise (Gen. 12:1ff). God had Abraham bring him a heifer, a goat, and a ram, and cut them in half (Gen. 15:10). Later that evening 'when the sun had gone down and it was dark, behold, a smoking fire pot and a flaming torch passed between these pieces' (Gen. 15:17). What is the significance of these events? The subsequent verse provides an answer from the immediate context: 'On that day the LORD made a covenant with Abram' (Gen. 15:18). In this connection O. Palmer Robertson comments that

> by dividing animals and passing between the pieces, participants in a covenant pledged themselves to life and death. These actions established an oath of self-malediction. If they should break the commitment involved in the covenant, they were asking that their own bodies be torn in pieces just as the animals had been divided ceremonially.[26]

There is confirmation of this interpretation in the prophet Jeremiah:

> And the men who transgressed my covenant and did not keep the terms of the covenant that they made before me, I will make them like the calf that they cut in two and passed between its parts. ... Their dead bodies shall be food for the birds of the air and the beasts of the earth (34:18-20).

---

[26]O. Palmer Robertson, *Christ of the Covenants* (Phillipsburg: P & R, 1980), p. 130; also Wenham, p. 332; Kidner, pp. 124-25; Sarna, pp. 114-15; Waltke, pp. 243-45; cf. Walton, p. 423.

In other words, when parties cut a covenant they severed animals, indicative of what would happen to either party for violating the terms of the covenant.[27] There are echoes of this practice in the inauguration of the Mosaic covenant when Moses sprinkled blood upon the people (Exod. 24:8). As Robertson observes, 'this blood of sprinkling symbolized not only the cleansing of the people. It also consecrated them to keep the covenant on pain of death.'[28] Confirmation of this conclusion is made clear in the repetition of the curses attached to the respective covenants, namely, the presence of the vultures that eat the carcasses of the severed animals (cf. Gen. 15:11; Jer. 34:20; Exod. 24:7). In the New Testament's interpretation of these events, their relationship to the second Adam becomes more apparent.

New Testament connection to Genesis 15:1ff

In Hebrews 9:15-20 the author alludes to the events of Genesis 15:1ff. Christ 'is the mediator of a new covenant, so that those who are called may receive the promised eternal inheritance, since a death has occurred that redeems them from the transgressions committed under the first covenant' (Heb. 9:15). Now, to be sure, the 'first covenant' refers to the Mosaic covenant, not the Abrahamic.[29] Nevertheless, what applies to the inauguration of the Mosaic covenant also applies to the Abrahamic covenant; the former is founded upon the latter (Exod. 2:24). Moreover, the same inauguration rites apply to both – cutting a covenant with the shedding of blood, represented by the severed animals with Abraham and the sprinkling of blood with Moses. This is

---

[27]See Vos, *Biblical Theology*, p. 86; Meredith Kline, *By Oath Consigned* (Grand Rapids: Eerdmans, 1956), p. 17; Delbert R. Hillers, *Covenant: The History of a Biblical Idea* (1969; Baltimore: Johns Hopkins University Press, 1982), pp. 102-03; see e.g. 'Treaty of Esharhaddon with Baal of Tyre,' 41. (425), in *ANE* 2, p. 63.

[28]Robertson, *Christ of the Covenants*, p. 135.

[29]Lane, *Hebrews*, p. 242; Ellingworth, *Hebrews*, p. 461.

established by an examination of Hebrews 9:17: διαθήκη γὰρ ἐπὶ νεκροῖς βεβαία (diathêkê gar epi nekrois bebaia), lit. 'a covenant is made firm over dead bodies' (cf. Gen. 15:9-21; Exod. 24:3-8; Ps. 50:5, esp. LXX; Jer. 34:17-20).[30] This means that Hebrews 9:15-20 refers to the covenant headship of the second Adam. Just as God brought the curse of self-malediction upon himself in his covenant promise to Abraham, so too the author of Hebrews writes that Christ has borne the covenant curses upon himself for those under the Mosaic covenant. The line of covenants, Noahic, Abrahamic, and Mosaic, are rooted in the protological covenant promise of the Gospel, the *protoevangelium* (Gen. 3:15). The death of the second Adam therefore

> is to be understood in terms of the long history of God's dealing with his people. By hearing the full consequences of covenantal pledge-to-death, Christ delivers from the curse of the covenant. No remission from guilty transgression could be gained without the shedding of blood. Christ therefore presented his body as the sacrificial victim of the covenantal curse.[31]

This means that the work of the second Adam is intimately connected with the failed work of the first. What Genesis 3:15 said in seminal form is that the second Adam would deliver the people of God from the curse of sin and death, a reality that has been progressively revealed in each of the subsequent major covenants in redemptive history.

The promise of the *protoevangelium* culminates in the events surrounding the crucifixion, beginning with the second Adam saying: 'For this is my blood of the covenant, which is poured out for many for

---

[30]Robertson, *Christ of the Covenants*, p. 142. Lane similarly translates v. 17: 'For a covenant is made legally secure on the basis of sacrificial victims' (Lane, *Hebrews*, pp. 229, 242-43; cf. Ellingworth, *Hebrews*, pp. 462-65.

[31]Robertson, *Christ of the Covenants*, p. 144.

the forgiveness of sins' (Matt. 26:28; cf. Exod. 24:8; Jer. 31:31-34). Adam's post-fall vestments were not only a priestly covering reminding man of his sin, but they also pointed forward to the sacrifice, the shedding of blood, of the second Adam. This theme is repeated throughout the Noahic, Abrahamic, and Mosaic covenants in the altar, tabernacle, and temple worship. Further connections to protology can be seen just prior to Christ's crucifixion. Scholars have noted that Christ's crucifixion takes place on Friday, the sixth day of the week, the same day on which Adam was created. In a twist of irony, Pilate stands before the crowds and cries out, 'Behold the man!' (John 19:5), echoing the creation of Adam. Christ completed the work that he had been sent to do (John 17:4), which ends in his cry from the cross, Τετέλεσται (tetelestai), 'It is finished!' (John 19:30), corresponding to the completion of the creation on the sixth day (cf. Gen. 2:1-2, LXX).[32] Following this, there was a day of rest, a Sabbath (John 19:31), and then, 'on the first day of the week' (John 20.1) Christ arose from the dead. Regarding this chain of events and their parallels in Genesis 1-2, N. T. Wright comments 'that Jesus' public career is to be understood as the completion of the original creation, with the resurrection as the start of the new.'[33] Affirmation of this overall trajectory is seen in the tearing of the veil in the temple immediately following Christ's death (Matt. 27:51; Heb. 6:19; 9:3; 10:20).[34]

---

[32]Genesis 2.1-2 (LXX) uses the term συντελέω (sunteleô) twice in connection with the completion of the work of day six.

[33]N. T. Wright, *The Resurrection of the Son of God* (Minneapolis: Fortress, 2003), p. 440; similarly F. F. Bruce, *The Gospel of John* (1983; Grand Rapids: Eedrmans, 1992), p. 359; cf. Herman Ridderbos, *The Gospel of John* (Grand Rapids: Eerdmans, 1997), p. 601.

[34]William Hendriksen, *Matthew*, NTC (1974; Grand Rapids: Baker,1995), p. 974; Donald A. Hagner, *Matthew 14-28*, WBC, vol. 33b (Dallas: Word, 1995), pp. 848-49.

In Genesis 3:24 God placed two cherubim at the eastern entrance to the garden of Eden prohibiting entrance into the archetypal temple. In the subsequent tabernacle and temple these two cherubim were represented by embroidered figures on the veil or curtain that separated the outer temple from the holy of holies (Exod. 26:31-33). No one could enter the holy of holies at will, unless it was the high priest at the appointed time (e.g. Lev. 16:1ff). Now that the penalty for the curse had been paid and the promise of the *protoevangelium* had arrived, at the dawn of the new creation the cherubim no longer stand guard at the entrance barring access under the penalty of death. Because the veil has been torn in two, the cherubim have withdrawn to their station before the throne of God (Rev. 4:6-8) and the new adamic humanity may once again enter into the divine presence. What about the connections that exist with the resurrection of Christ, the dawn of the new creation?

The resurrection of Christ

When one examines the third aspect of Christ's work, namely, his resurrection from the dead, he is once again confronted with protology. The *locus classicus* in Scripture concerning Christ's resurrection from the dead is 1 Corinthians 15. The entire chapter finds its roots in protology, Genesis 1–3.[35] In particular, the protological bedrock of 1 Corinthians 15 is evident in the following two sections: (1) vv. 20-28; and (2) vv. 35-49.

1 Corinthians 15:20-28

In verses 20-28, Genesis 1:26-28 and 3:17-19, which detail the creation of Adam and his subsequent fall, lie just below the surface. This is evident when Paul writes: 'For as by a man came death, by a man has come also the resurrection of the dead. For as in Adam all die, so

---

[35]Wright, *Resurrection*, pp. 334, 346, 360.

also in Christ shall all be made alive' (vv. 21-22). Clearly, Paul establishes a parallel between the death brought by the first Adam and the resurrection from death brought by the second Adam. Moreover, as in Romans 5:12-19, there is a clear line of demarcation between the imputed guilt and its consequent, death, of Adam and the imputed righteousness and its consequent, eternal life, of Christ. There is a further connection between Adam and Christ when Paul quotes Psalm 8:6 in connection with the resurrection of Christ: 'For "God has put all things in subjection under his feet." But when it says, "all things are put in subjection," it is plain that he is excepted who put all things in subjection under him' (v. 27). Paul draws upon the dominion mandate of Genesis 1:26-27; God placed all things under Adam's feet, yet man abandoned his divine vocation.

As previously stated, God's intended goal for the creation has not changed; the dominion mandate was repeated in each of the three major covenants. Moreover, the mandate remained the same throughout redemptive history and awaited the arrival of the second Adam, who would take up the abandoned work of the first Adam. Along these lines Wright observes that

> just as, when Israel failed to be the light-bearing people for the world, the covenant God did not rewrite the vocation but rather sent the Messiah to act in Israel's place ... so now the failure of humankind ('Adam') to be the creator's wise, image-bearing steward over creation has not led the creator to rewrite the vocation, but rather to send the Messiah as the truly human being.

Unlike the first Adam, the second Adam rules the world in obedience to God the Father (Pss. 2, 72, 89).[36] Taking

---

[36]Wright, *Resurrection*, pp. 334, 336; see also Vos, *Biblical Theology*, p. 386; Schreiner, *Paul*, pp. 175-76; James D. G. Dunn, *The Theology of Paul the Apostle* (Grand Rapids: Eerdmans, 1998), p. 241.

into consideration verse 23 and the implications of the resurrection of Christ, there are important connections to the last Adam and the new adamic humanity: 'But each in his own order: Christ the firstfruits, then at his coming those who belong to Christ.' Paul states that Christ is the firstfruits of the resurrection harvest (cf. Exod. 23:16, 19) and that the rest of the harvest will occur at the *parousia* of Christ. The implication is that the new creation will arise out of the old by the resurrection of the new adamic humanity who bear the image of the last Adam and fulfill God's intended purpose for the creation – spreading the image of God unto the ends of the earth (Rom. 8:29; Phil. 2:6-11; 3:20-21).[37]

1 Corinthians 15:35-49
Once again the key to a proper comprehension of verses 35-49 lies in protology, Genesis 1–2. Paul expressly makes this connection when he writes: 'Just as we have borne the image of the man of dust, we shall also bear the image of the man of heaven' (v. 49). In the passage one finds the major themes of Genesis 1–2. In verses 36-38 Paul speaks of seeds and plants, day three of the creation week;[38] in verse 39 he writes of the bodies of man, fish, and birds, day five; and in verse 41 he writes of the astral bodies, the sun, moon, and stars, day four. Paul implicitly speaks of the work of the Holy Spirit in connection with the new adamic humanity. Just as the Holy Spirit was present at the creation hovering like a bird over the chaotic waters (Gen. 1:2), symbolically represented in Noah's dove (Gen. 8:8-11), present in the pillar of cloud in the exodus like a bird (Deut. 32:11; Exod. 13:21-22; Hag. 2:5; Isa. 63:11), and

---

[37]Wright, *Resurrection*, p. 337; also Ridderbos, *Paul*, p. 225.

[38]Paul does not appeal to day three in terms of biology in connection to seed-bearing trees and plants but rather draws a christological, soteriological, and eschatological connection. This once again demonstrates how the NT interprets Genesis 1–3 in contradistinction to popular approaches.

present in the form of a dove at the inauguration of the ministry of the second Adam as he too emerged from the waters (Luke 3:22), so too the Holy Spirit in conjunction with the new Adam is the one who gives life to this new humanity: 'Thus it is written, "The first man Adam became a living being"; the last Adam became a life-giving Spirit' (v. 45; cf. Gen. 2:7; Rom. 1:4).[39] The first creation is tied to the first Adam, and the new heavens and earth and its birth is tied to the resurrection of the second Adam. As Richard Gaffin points out, 'All soteric experience involves existence in the new creation age, inaugurated by his resurrection.'[40]

One may summarize the protological and christological connections in 1 Corinthians 15 with the comments of James Dunn:

> Christ is the last Adam, prototype of God's new human creation, in accord with the original blueprint. On the other hand, he is on the side of God, co-regent with God, co-lifegiver with the Spirit. And in between he is God's Son, whose sonship is shared with those who believe in him, the elder brother of a new family, firstborn from the dead. Yet he is also Son of God in power. And he is Lord, whose lordship both completes the intended dominion of Adam and exercises divine prerogatives.[41]

At this point in the survey of the work of the second Adam, clear connections between protology and christology have emerged. The life, death, and resurrection of Christ

---

[39]Modified ESV; Wright, *Resurrection*, pp. 341-42. This is not to say that Paul sees Christ and the Holy Spirit as one in the same but that the two persons work in conjunction to produce the new Adamic humanity (contra Dunn, *Paul*, pp. 261-62; cf. Gordon D. Fee, *God's Empowering Presence* [Peabody: Henrickson, 1994], p. 266-67; C.K. Barret, *The First Epistle to the Corinthians*, BNTC [1968; Peabody: Henrickson, 1996], p. 374).

[40]Richard B. Gaffin, Jr., *Resurrection and Redemption* (1978; Phillipsburg: P & R, 1987), p. 138.

[41]Dunn, *Paul*, p. 265.

find their genesis in the failed work of the first Adam. There is still yet another connection between protology and christology, namely, the helpmate of the second Adam, the second Eve.

The second Adam's helpmate

When God first created Adam, he recognized that it was not good for the man to be alone (Gen. 2:18). God set out to create a helper for Adam that resulted in the creation of woman (Gen. 2:21-22). Upon seeing the woman Adam broke forth into poetic exclamation: 'Then the man said, "This at last is bone of my bones and flesh of my flesh; she shall be called Woman, because she was taken out of Man" ' (Gen. 2:23). To this poetic exclamation, the narrator adds the comment: 'Therefore a man shall leave his father and his mother and hold fast to his wife, and they shall become one flesh' (Gen. 2:24). The account of the creation of woman is not primarily to do with biology and the number of ribs that a man has in comparison to a woman, nor is it only about marriage. Rather, the account of the creation of the woman has its telos in Christ. This is most evident in Paul's epistle to the Ephesians. In his explanation of marriage, Paul quotes Genesis 2:24 and then states: 'This mystery is profound, and I am saying that it refers to Christ and the church' (Eph. 5:32). What is the significance of the term 'mystery' or μυστήριον (mustêrion)? Μυστήριον is a technical term in Paul's language that refers to that which was once hidden but now revealed.[42] This definition is evident when Paul states that he was preaching the gospel of Christ, 'according to the revelation of the mystery that was kept secret for long ages but has now been disclosed and through the prophetic writings has been made known to all nations' (Rom. 16:25-26). This means that Genesis 2:24, the full meaning of which having been previously unknown, has now been revealed to speak

---

[42]Colin Brown, 'μυστήριον' in NIDNTT, vol. 3, p. 504; Andrew T. Lincoln, *Ephesians*, WBC, vol. 42 (Dallas: Word, 1990), p. 381.

not just of marriage but of the relationship between Christ and the Church, linking protology, christology, and now, ecclesiology.

In his explanation of the relationship between Christ and the Church, Paul draws the analogy between the authority of Christ and that of the husband and the submission of the Church and that of the wife (Eph. 5:22-27). This husband and wife imagery appears especially in the book of Revelation: 'And I saw the holy city, new Jerusalem, coming down out of heaven from God, prepared as a bride adorned for her husband' (Rev. 21:2).

These two passages provide important information regarding the function and role of the Church. Recall that Paul said that Adam was a type of the one to come (Rom. 5:14). Given Paul's interpretation of Genesis 2:24, this logically requires that Eve is a type of the Church (cf. Isa. 54:5-8; Jer. 21:1-3; 31:31-32; Ezek. 16:8-14; 23; Hos. 1-3; Mark 2:18-20; John 3:29). O'Brien comments that 'it was God's intention from the beginning when he instituted marriage to picture the relationship between Christ and his redeemed people'.[43] Just as Adam needed a helpmate to complete the covenant of works, namely, the dominion mandate, so too Christ has a helpmate to carry out his labors as the second Adam. How does the second Adam fulfill the dominion mandate, and what role does the second Eve play?

The dominion mandate

Genesis 1:28 gives Adam the task of (1) spreading the image of God throughout the earth; (2) extending the temple to the ends of the earth; (3) exercising dominion through elements 1 and 2; and (4) accomplishing this task with the assistance of his helpmate. Adam and Eve were unable to fulfill the dominion mandate because of their sin. Each subsequent republication of the mandate

---

[43]So Peter T. O'Brien, *The Letter to the Ephesians*, PNTC (Grand Rapids: Eerdmans, 1999), pp. 435, 438.

in the Noahic, Abrahamic, and Mosaic covenants was not an effort to remand or re-administer it to man but a typological signpost of the second Adam – the one who would fulfill the abandoned work of the first Adam. That the second Adam fulfills the dominion mandate is something that many do not grasp.

The dominion mandate misunderstood

Surveying popular conservative evangelical literature on the dominion mandate, the fall of Adam and, more importantly, the work of Christ are not taken into consideration together. Douglas Wilson, for example, writes that

> marriage was created by God to provide companionship in the labor of dominion. The cultural mandate, the requirement to fill and subdue the earth, is still in force, and a husband cannot fulfill this portion of the task in isolation. He needs a companion suitable for him in the work to which God has called him.[44]

The impression one gets from Wilson's statement is that the fall has had no effect upon the original dominion mandate. This interpretive trajectory even finds representation in scholarly writings.

John Murray argues that the 'creation ordinances of procreation, replenishing the earth, subduing the earth, dominion over the creatures, labor, marriage, and the sabbath are not abrogated.' Now, while Murray does take the fall into account, he does not connect the dominion mandate to the work of Christ. For example, concerning procreation Murray writes that

> we have found that there is no suspension of this institution but rather repeated emphasis upon it. The entrance of sin into the world radically affected the

---

[44]Douglas Wilson, *Reforming Marriage* (Moscow: Canon Press, 1995), p. 19.

conditions under which it was to be exercised but, however aggravated these conditions of curse and travail are, they do not remove the obligation to be fruitful and multiply: they rather intensify the necessity or urge to its exercise.[45]

Murray goes on to quote Psalm 127:3-5 in connection with the dominion mandate: 'Behold, children are a heritage from the LORD, the fruit of the womb a reward. ... Blessed is the man who fills his quiver with them.'

It should be no surprise, then, that in popular literature one finds writers who argue that Christians must have large families in order to fulfill the dominion mandate. In this vein William Einwechter writes that

> the fulfillment of the dominion mandate cannot take place unless the prior commands of God recorded in v. 28 are observed: 'be fruitful and multiply and replenish the earth.' These two imperatives precede in time and in logical sequence the command to take dominion in the earth. Note the progression: 1) man must be *fruitful* and multiply so that, 2) he can *fill* the earth so that, 3) he can *have dominion* over all the earth. Thus, we see that fruitfulness in regard to bearing children is essential to the fulfillment of the dominion mandate! It is significant to recognize that the first commandment given to man in the Bible is the command to 'be fruitful and multiply.' This command is based on the institution of marriage (*cf. Gen. 2:18-24*), and it places marriage and the procreation of many children (*i.e.* a large family) at the center of God's purpose for man in the dominion mandate.[46]

Einwechter does not take the fall into consideration and presents the dominion mandate as if all that

---

[45]John Murray, *Principles of Conduct* (1957; Grand Rapids: Eerdmans, 2001), pp. 42, 78.

[46]William Einwechter, 'Children and the Dominion Mandate (Part 1),' *Chalcedon Report*, November (1998).

Christians must do is to have large families. Once again, Genesis 1:28 is interpreted in isolation from the work of Christ and the fall.

Another interpretation of the dominion mandate has been offered in connection with postmillennial eschatology. Kenneth Gentry writes that the dominion mandate, what he calls the 'Cultural Mandate,' was 'given at creation *before* the Fall, but it remains in effect even *after* the entry of sin.' Gentry sees the cultural mandate repeated in Psalm 8:4-6. He then connects the cultural mandate to the 'optimistic expectations of postmillennialism.' He writes that 'postmillennialism expects the world as a system (*kosmos*) to be brought under submission to God's rule by the active, sanctified agency of redeemed man, who has been renewed in the image of God (Col. 3:10; Eph. 4:24).'[47] Now, while Gentry factors in the fall and the soteric implications of the work of Christ, he still removes Christ from the picture. In Gentry's view the Church, the helpmate, the second Eve, not the second Adam, is the one who fulfills the dominion mandate.

Still yet, Henry Morris makes the argument that the dominion mandate is still in force and must be carried out, not by Christians, but by nations:

God's primeval dominion mandate (Gen. 1:26-28) has never been withdrawn, and thus is still in effect. It was given originally to Adam and Eve, then confirmed and expanded to Noah after the great Flood. It is, therefore, appropriate to raise the question as to how well the dominion mandate is being implemented by the present nations.[48]

---

[47]Kenneth L. Gentry, Jr., *He Shall Have Dominion* (1992; Tyler: Institute for Christian Economics, 1997), pp. 187-88.

[48]Henry Morris, 'God's Dominion Mandate and the Nations Today,' *Back to Genesis* 171a / March (2003).

While these five authors have varying doctrinal commitments, what they all have in common is that: (1) they make reference to the dominion mandate as if sin never entered the world; and (2) they fail to examine the dominion mandate with full appreciation and integration of the light of the revelation and work of the second Adam.

The dominion mandate correctly understood

While the aforementioned authors are correct to argue that the dominion mandate is still in effect, they fail to interpret the dominion mandate in the light of the revelation and work of Christ as the second Adam. Though the dominion mandate was remanded to Noah, subsequent to his reception of the mandate Noah sinned and demonstrated his inability to fulfill the mandate, a fact amply illustrated in the tower of Babel judgment upon Noah's descendants (Gen. 11:1ff).[49] Hence, the dominion mandate does not have a terminus in Noah and the nations, as Morris argues. Subsequent to the tower of Babel judgment God begins again with yet another Adam of sorts, Abraham. The dominion mandate is once again remanded to this Adam: 'I will make of you a great nation, and I will bless you and make your name great, so that you will be a blessing. I will bless those who bless you, and him who dishonors you I will curse, and in you all the families of the earth shall be blessed' (Gen. 12:2-3). Recall how Paul interprets this republication of the dominion mandate: 'And the Scripture, foreseeing that God would justify the Gentiles by faith, preached the gospel beforehand to Abraham, saying, "In you shall all the nations be blessed"' (Gal. 3:8). The mandate is a promise, not a command, and therefore cannot be divorced from Christ, the second Adam, or the gospel.[50] This mandate–gospel

---

[49]Sarna, *Genesis*, p. 84; Wenham, *Genesis*, p. 242.

[50]James D. G. Dunn, *The Epistle to the Galatians*, BNTC (Peabody: Hendrickson, 1993), p. 165.

connection has important implications for a proper understanding of the dominion mandate as it relates to the work of the second Adam.

First, while the dominion mandate is still in effect, it is fulfilled, neither by the nations, nor by Christian husbands or wives, nor by the Church, but by the second Adam, by Christ. As demonstrated above, the second Adam has successfully passed his own probation in perfect obedience to the will of his Father, has paid the penalty for the broken covenant of works for the people of God through his death on the cross, and is now the firstborn from the dead by the power of the Holy Spirit, the cornerstone of the new creation. Christ has taken up the work of the dominion mandate and with the assistance of his helpmate, his bride, the second Eve, the Church, is now fulfilling it. In this connection Dunn explains why Paul cites Psalm 8:4-6 in 1 Corinthians 15:27:

> The logic of the use of Ps. 8:4-6 is plain. The psalmist was assumed to have described God's purpose in creating humankind. God's intention had been to give his human creation authority over the rest of his creation. The reference will no doubt have been primarily to Gen. 1:28: God created human male and female as the climax of his creation, and said to them, 'Be fruitful and multiply, fill the earth and subdue it, and have dominion over the fish of the sea and over the birds of the air and over every living thing that moves upon the earth.' By referring Ps. 8:6b to Jesus the clear implication is that this divine purpose was seen to have been fulfilled in the exaltation of Christ. In his exaltation to God's right hand Christ (at last) fulfilled human destiny. All things were at last being put in subjection under the feet of God's representative man.[51]

---

[51]Dunn, *Paul*, p. 201.

The dominion mandate is most clearly in the hands of the second Adam in the Great Commission.

Second, in the Great Commission Christ states: 'All authority in heaven and on earth has been given to me. Go therefore and make disciples of all nations' (Matt. 28:18b-19a). The connection between the dominion mandate as it is given to Abraham and the Great Commission becomes even more evident when one compares the language of the LXX to that of verse 19a. Genesis 22:18 parallels verse 19a:

In your offspring all the nations [πάντα τὰ ἔθνη / panta ta ethnê] of the earth shall be blessed.

Make disciples of all the nations [πάντα τὰ ἔθνη / panta ta ethnê].

Notice that the language of πάντα τὰ ἔθνη is repeated in both the dominion mandate promise to Abraham and in the Great Commission.[52] Hence, the dominion mandate is fulfilled by Christ, the second Adam, with the assistance of his helpmate, his bride, the Church. The Church has a secondary role behind that of her husband.

Third, the dominion mandate cannot be fulfilled simply by procreation or by having large families. The work of the second Adam cannot be divorced from the work of the dominion mandate. The original pronouncement of the dominion mandate was tied to procreation. Adam and his helpmate were to produce offspring who bore the image of their creator, filling the earth with those who worshiped God. Subsequent to the fall, Adam and Eve could no longer fulfill the mandate because of the presence of sin, as is evident in the battle between the seed of the serpent and the woman (Gen. 4:1ff). With the advent of the second Adam, Christ takes up the

---

[52]D. A. Carson, *Matthew 13-28*, EBC (Grand Rapids: Zondervan, 1995), p. 596.

work of the dominion mandate by producing offspring with his helpmate, the Church, and creates those who bear his image.[53] The dominion mandate is not fulfilled through procreation but through the propagation of the gospel. Therefore, those who are not married, such as Paul himself (1 Cor. 7:8), can boast of having many children (1 Cor. 4:14; Gal. 4:19; 1 Tim. 1:2; 2 Tim. 1:2; Philem. 10; Titus 1:4) because they are produced through the propagation of the gospel. They are not the offspring of a husband and wife but the offspring of the second Adam and his helpmate, the second Eve, the Church (cf. John 1:13). Does Christ successfully fulfill the dominion mandate?

The work of the second Adam completed

Pictures surface in various portions of Scripture that show that Christ is successful in fulfilling the dominion mandate. One such passage is Daniel 7. In Daniel 7 the prophet has a vision where he sees four beasts rise out of the sea: a lion with eagle's wings (v. 4), a bear (v. 5), a leopard (v. 6), and a dreadful and terrible beast, exceedingly strong (v. 7). Daniel sees the dominion of the four ferocious beasts taken away (v. 12), and one like the son of man comes on the clouds of heaven and 'to him was given dominion and glory and a kingdom' (v. 14). Daniel's vision describes the eschatological victory of Christ over those kingdoms that oppose him in protological terms, in terms of Genesis 1–2.[54] Daniel's vision is a repetition of Psalm 8, the completed creation and enthronement of man. Psalm 8 poetically echoes Genesis 1:26-28: 'What is man that you are mindful of him, and the son of man that you care for him? ... You have given him dominion over the works of your hands; you have put all things under his feet, all sheep and oxen, and also the beasts of the field, the birds of the heavens, and the fish of the sea' (vv. 4-8).[55] Daniel's

---

[53]Ridderbos, *Paul*, p. 81.
[54]E. J. Young, *Daniel* (Banner of Truth, 1949), pp. 155-56.

vision tells of the eschatological victory of Christ in terms of Psalm 8: the son of man comes and takes dominion from the beasts of the earth. The conclusion of all history is given in terms of the beginning of history, eschatology is recounted in protological terms. Or, the work of the second Adam is rooted in and mirrors the work of the first Adam (cf. Gen. 1:26-28; Ps. 8:4-8; Dan. 7; Rev. 13-14).[56] Stated simply, Daniel's vision is a visual rendition of Psalm 8. Similar protological language is used to describe the eschatological age and the work of Christ in John's apocalypse.

A description of the global extent of the results of Christ's work, for example, is found in the book of Revelation: 'And they sang a new song, saying: "Worthy are you to take the scroll and to open its seals, for you were slain, and by your blood you ransomed people for God from every tribe and language and people and nation"' (Rev. 5:9; 7:9). G. K. Beale explains that the new song 'associates Christ's redemptive work with the beginning of a new creation'. He draws this conclusion based on two factors: (1) this verse is within the context where God's creation is specifically mentioned in Revelation 4:11; and (2) the hymns of Revelation 5:12-13

---

[55] Joyce G. Baldwin, *Daniel*, TOTC (Downers Grove: Inter Varsity, 1978), p. 143.

[56] John E. Goldingay, *Daniel*, WBC, vol. 30 (Dallas: Word, 1989), pp. 188, 190. Wright comments that, 'Daniel was a favorite with Jews of the first century AD. One of the climactic moments in this book, arguably, is the scene in which the true Israel, seen in apocalyptic terms as a human figure, is exalted to a position of glory and authority over the mythical beasts who have been oppressing God's people. Whatever referents may have been in the mind of the original authors, there should be no doubt that in the first century many would read such imagery as referring to Israel and the nations, and would hear in the background the overtones of Genesis 2. Divine order will be restored to the creator's garden, through a genuine Adam – i.e. Israel – who will renounce idolatry and so, in obedience to the creator, rule wisely over the creation' (N. T. Wright, *The New Testament and the People of God* [Minneapolis: Fortress, 1992], p. 266).

are explicitly paralleled with the hymn of 4:11 and God's work of creation. The 'myriads of myriads and thousands of thousands' (Rev. 5:11) of image bearers sing:

> 'Worthy is the Lamb who was slain, to receive power and wealth and wisdom and might and honor and glory and blessing!' And I heard every creature in heaven and on earth and under the earth and in the sea, and all that is in them, saying, 'To him who sits on the throne and to the Lamb be blessing and honor and glory and might forever and ever!' (Rev. 5:12-13).[57]

Images similar to the one above are found in other parts of Scripture.

In looking at the results of the consummated kingdom, from the Psalms one reads that Christ will 'have dominion from sea to sea, and from the river to the ends of the earth' (Ps. 72:8).[58] Likewise the prophet Isaiah writes concerning Israel as God's servant, a reality that finds its ultimate significance in the work of Christ: 'It is too light a thing that you should be my servant to raise up the tribes of Jacob and to bring back the preserved of Israel; I will make you as a light for the nations, that my salvation may reach to the ends of the earth' (Isa. 49:6; cf. John 8:12).[59] Clearly, Christ will fulfill the dominion mandate – he will produce offspring that bear his image, the image of God, and fill the new creation to the ends of the earth. The second Adam will extend the temple to the ends of the earth as well, the second aspect of the dominion mandate.

Inherent in the original dominion mandate is the idea of extending the temple to the ends of the earth. That

---

[57]G. K. Beale, *The Book of Revelation*, NIGTC (Grand Rapids: Eerdmans, 1999), p. 358.

[58]Derek Kidner, *Psalms 1-72*, TOTC (Downers Grove: Inter Varsity Press, 1973), p. 256.

[59]E. J. Young, *The Book of Isaiah*, vol. 3 (1972: Grand Rapids: Eerdmans, 1997), pp. 273-74.

the second Adam will accomplish this goal emerges quite clearly once in the book of Revelation:

> Then I saw a new heaven and a new earth, for the first heaven and the first earth had passed away, and the sea was no more. And I saw the holy city, the new Jerusalem, coming down out of heaven from God, prepared as a bride adorned for her husband. And I heard a loud voice from the throne saying, 'Behold, the dwelling place of God is with man. He will dwell with them, and they will be his people, and God himself will be with them as their God' (Rev. 21:1-3).

Here multifaceted protological imagery reappears at the conclusion of redemptive history. A new heaven and earth surfaces, for the first heaven and earth, the domain of the first Adam, have been superseded by the domain of the eschatological Adam.[60] In the first heaven and earth the creation of the sun, moon, and stars were

---

[60]It is important to note the Qumran understanding of eschatology and the connection to Genesis. The Qumran community read Genesis not in terms of science but in terms of eschatology. For example: 'For God has chosen them for an everlasting Covenant and all the glory of Adam shall be theirs' (1QS 4); and, 'Thou wilt cast away all their sins. Thou wilt cause them to inherit all the glory of Adam and abundance of days' (1QH 4 [17] Hymn 1 [23]); and, 'To the penitents of the desert who, saved, shall live for a thousand generations and to whom all the glory of Adam shall belong, as also to their seed for ever' (4 Q171 3). This same hope and connection between protology, soteriology, and eschatology is present in early Jewish thought. One can contrast the following statements, that of Adam immediately after the fall, 'What is this thou hast done to me, because I have been deprived of the glory with which I was clothed' (*Apoc. Moses*, *ANF*, vol. 8 [1886; Grand Rapids: Eerdmans, 1995], p. 567); with the eschatological hope of Adam and Eve: 'For it will not happen to thee now, but at the last times. Then shall arise all flesh from Adam even to that great day, as many as shall be a holy people; then shall be given to them all the delight of paradise, and God shall be in the midst of them' (*Apoc. Moses*, p. 566). One finds similar imagery in intertestamental Judaism (see 4 Esdras 7.122-25; see James D. G. Dunn, *The Theology of Paul the Apostle* [Grand Rapids: Eerdmans, 1998], p. 93, n. 69).

primarily for the marking of time (Gen. 1:9-19). In the new heavens and earth, however, there is 'no need of sun or moon to shine on it, for the glory of God gives it light, and its lamp is the Lamb' (Rev. 21:23; cf. Isa. 60:19; Ezek. 43:2-5).[61] Just as God brought to the first Adam his bride, so too the bride of the second Adam, the second Eve, the Church, appears. What is different, however, is that unlike the garden-temple where God was separated from his image bearers, God now has his temple in and among the new adamic humanity (1 Cor. 6:19; Eph. 2:19-22; 1 Pet. 2:5; Rev. 21:22); the temple is actually God dwelling in the midst of the new adamic humanity both spatially and spiritually.[62] The great extent of the eschatological temple is represented in its symbolic size and proportions.

The holy city, new Jerusalem, the eschatological temple, is 12,000 cubic stadia in length, breadth, and height – a perfect cube. A *stadia* is approximately 607 feet; therefore the temple is approximately 1,400 miles long, high, and wide (Rev. 21:16; cf. NLT). The walls that surround the massive eschatological temple are 144 cubits in thickness, or approximately 216 feet thick (Rev. 21:17; cf. NLT). On the dimensions of the eschatological temple Beale explains that 'surprisingly, the size of the city is apparently the approximated size of the then known Hellenistic world. This suggests further that the temple-city represents not merely the glorified saints of Israel but the redeemed from all nations, who are considered to be true, spiritual Israelites.'[63] The second Adam accomplishes the dominion mandate by extending the temple, which is also the people of God, to the ends

---

[61]Beale, *Revelation*, pp. 1039-48.

[62]Beale, *Revelation*, p. 1046. In this vein it is interesting to note that the Qumran community looked for this same reality: 'He has commanded that a Sanctuary of men be built for Himself, that there they may send up, like the smoke of incense, the works of the Law' (4 Q174).

[63]Beale, *Revelation*, p. 1074.

of the earth.[64] These protological echoes are not the only elements that reappear at the consummation of the completed work of the second Adam.

Once again, embedded protological elements resurface in the closing chapters of John's apocalypse.[65] The eschatological temple is situated on a 'high mountain' (Rev. 21:10), as were the archetypal temple and subsequent worship sites in the Old Testament (Gen. 2:10-14; Ezek. 28:14, 16; Exod. 3:1; Ps. 48:1-2). As the river of Eden flowed out to water the garden (Gen. 2:10), so too a pure river of water of life flows out of the eschatological temple (Rev. 22:1). Likewise, the tree of life (Gen. 2:9) reappears in the eschatological temple: 'Through the middle of the street of the city; also, on either side of the river, the tree of life with its twelve kinds of fruit, yielding its fruit each month. The leaves of the tree were for the healing of the nations' (Rev. 22:2).[66] The precious stones and metals that adorned the garden temple, the tabernacle, and Solomon's temple also appear in the eschatological temple (cf. Rev. 21:18-20; Gen. 2:10-14; Ezek. 28:13; Exod. 25:11, 17, 24, 29, 36; 28:7-10).[67]

The inhabitants of the eschatological temple also perform the same priestly functions as Adam did in the

---

[64]There are protological and eschatological connections once again in the Qumran community: 'I shall accept them and they shall be my people and I shall be for them for ever. I will dwell with them for ever and ever and will sanctify my [sa]nctuary by my glory. I will cause my glory to rest on it until the day of creation on which I shall create my sanctuary, establishing it for myself for all time according to the covenant which I have made with Jacob in Bethel' (2 QT = 2Q19, 20 19, ln. 7-10). Cf. G. K. Beale, 'Temple Garden,' *Kerux* 18/2 (2003), p. 28.

[65]Rabbinic interpretation also makes connections between protology and eschatology. They place the righteous in the garden of Eden able to see the wicked in Gehenna (see *Mid. Rabb.* Lev. 32.1; cf. Num. 13.2).

[66]Rabbinic interpretation saw the righteous eating from the tree of life in the eschaton (see *Mid. Rabb.* Exo. 25.8).

[67]Beale, *Revelation*, pp. 1103-11. Scripture casts the eschaton in terms of protology (see Ezek. 36.35; also Beale, 'Garden Temple,' p. 38).

garden-temple. Adam was instructed to work and keep the garden (Gen. 2:15). As has been previously explained, this is priestly language (Num. 3:7-8; cf. 4:23-24, 26). Likewise, the new adamic humanity serves God in the eschatological temple, though they serve him having been redeemed from the curse of Genesis 3:16-19: 'And there shall be no more curse, but the throne of God and of the lamb shall be in it, and his servants shall serve him' (Rev. 22:3; NKJV).[68] Once again the servants of God shall see the face of God (Rev. 22:4) as Adam and Eve once beheld his face (Gen. 3:8; MT). There is a significant difference, however, between the dress of the first priest, Adam, and that of the new humanity. Adam and Eve were naked when they served God in the garden-temple (Gen. 2:25). The new adamic humanity, however, will never appear naked before God. Instead, they are clothed in the righteousness of Christ as a permanent reminder and source of praise for the work of the second Adam (Rev. 3:18; 19:8).

It is essential that one sees the completed work of Christ in Revelation in terms of the failed work of the first Adam. Beale notes this connection in an excellent summary:

> The Garden of Eden was the first temple ... not only was Adam to 'guard' this sanctuary but he was to subdue the earth, according to Gen. 1:28: 'And God blessed them ... "Be fruitful and multiply, and fill the earth, and subdue it; and rule over the fish of the sea and over the birds of the sky, and over every living thing that creeps on the surface."' As Adam was to begin to rule over and subdue the earth, it is plausible to suggest that he was to extend the geographical boundaries of the garden until Eden extended throughout and covered the whole earth. This meant the presence of God, which was initially limited to Eden, was to be extended throughout

---

[68]Beale, *Revelation*, p. 1112; also Meredith Kline, *Kingdom Prologue* (Overland Park: Two Age Press, 2000), pp. 48-49.

the whole earth. What Adam failed to do, Revelation pictures Christ as finally having done. The Edenic imagery beginning in Rev. 22:1 reflects an intention to show that the building of the temple, which began in Genesis 2, will be completed in Christ and his people and will encompass the whole new creation.[69]

Conclusion

Having examined the work of Christ and the important connections between protology and christology, the similarities between the first and second Adams have been made clear: the protological aspects in the life, death, and resurrection of Christ, the relationship between protology and ecclesiology, and the connections to eschatology, namely, the dominion mandate and the completed work of the second Adam. In all of these areas, the interpretive and irrefragable relationship between protology and the other doctrinal loci has been demonstrated. At this point in the investigation, there is one last protological issue remaining, namely, the Sabbath and its relationship to the work of the second Adam.

---

[69]Beale, *Revelation*, p. 1111.

6

The Sabbath

Introduction

The contexts and the work of both the first and second Adams have been examined, and the investigation has demonstrated the connections between protology, christology, and ecclesiology. In the previous chapter, the relationship between protology and christology as it especially relates to eschatology was only briefly explained. The finished work of the second Adam as it relates to the dominion mandate was explored, namely, by beginning the new creation, by filling the new creation with those who bear the image of God, and by extending the temple, or the sacred space, to the ends of the earth. What has not been investigated is protology and the work of the second Adam as it relates to sacred time, namely the Sabbath. One must understand the nature of the seventh day of creation (Gen. 2:1-3) as it relates to the first Adam, to Israel, the typological son of God, and to the second Adam. Bound up in the protological Sabbath is the doctrine of eschatology. Consequently, the relationship of the Sabbath to Adam, Israel, and Christ will be explored. In this chapter, one must see how eschatology is not rooted in days immediately preceding the return of Christ as with dispensationalism, but how eschatology has its radix in protology, in pre-redemptive history, in Genesis 1–2. Recognizing that eschatology precedes, temporally and logically, soteriology, one's understanding of the relationship of eschatology to the rest of the doctrinal loci must necessarily change. The investigation must therefore begin with an examination of Adam's relationship to the Sabbath.

Adam and the Sabbath

At the conclusion of the creation week, after six days of labor, God rested on the seventh day, blessed it and sanctified it. God rested from his labors, and it was now Adam's duty to follow his heavenly Father's example, by performing his own labors of the covenant of works, by multiplying the image of God, by extending the temple to the ends of the earth, and by entering into the rest of God. In this connection Geerhardus Vos writes that the covenant of works 'was nothing but an embodiment of the Sabbatical principle'.[1] What is the sabbatical principle? It is the idea that there was a terminus, an eschatological goal, to Adam's labors. Vos observes that 'in so far as the covenant of works posited for mankind an absolute goal and unchangeable future, the eschatological may be even said to have preceded the soteric religion.'[2] In other words, eschatology appears in pre-redemptive history prior to the entrance of sin and therefore prior to the need for soteriology.

Suffice it to say that God placed an eschatological goal before Adam, and that goal was sacramentally represented in the tree of life. If Adam had been obedient, he would have carried out the work of the covenant and perhaps have eaten from the tree of life, permanently securing eternal life. The exact relationship between the tree of life, Adam's work, and the eschatological rest of the seventh day is unknown. One may surmise that Adam would have performed the labors of the covenant of works and with each passing Sabbath rested from his labors in anticipation of the completion of his work and

---

[1] Geerhardus Vos, *Biblical Theology* (1948; Edinburgh: Banner of Truth, 1996), p. 140.

[2] Geerhardus Vos, *The Pauline Eschatology* (1930; Phillipsburg: P & R, 1994), p. 325, n. 1.

entrance into the eternal seventh day rest of God. Adam did not enter the eternal Sabbath rest of God by his own labors due to his rebellion in the garden-temple. Adam's fall, however, did not negate the eschatological goal of the covenant of works. Recall that God did not rewrite the vocation of the first Adam but sent another to act in Adam's place.[3] God did not change the eschatological goal of the covenant of works but rather sent another who would faithfully perform the work and enter the rest of the seventh day. What this means is that the Sabbath, as sacred time, serves as a temporal eschatological sign of the covenant of works, a temporal reminder of the goal of creation.[4] Due to the presence of eschatology being imbedded in protology, the Sabbath principle continues throughout redemptive history. This relationship between protology and eschatology is evident in God's covenant with Israel.

Israel and the Sabbath

In the Mosaic covenant the seventh day rest re-emerges on the landscape of history. The Sabbath is published in what most know as the fourth commandment of the Decalogue:

> You shall not take the name of the LORD your God in vain, for the LORD will not hold him guiltless who takes his name in vain. Remember the Sabbath day, to keep it holy. Six days you shall labor, and do all your work, but the seventh day is a Sabbath to the LORD your God. On it you shall not do any work, you, or your son, or your daughter, your male servant, or your female servant, or your livestock, or the sojourner who is within your gates. For in six days the LORD made heaven and earth, the sea, and all that is in them, and rested the seventh

---

[3] N. T. Wright, *The Resurrection of the Son of God* (Minneapolis: Fortress, 2003), p. 334.

[4] Rabbinic interpretation likens the world to come to the Sabbath (see *Mid. Rabb.* Ruth 3.3).

day. Therefore the LORD blessed the Sabbath day and made it holy (Exod. 20:7-11).

Along with the publication of the Sabbath command there is an explicit protological connection, the creation week. The question that one must answer is, What function does the Sabbath serve in relation to Israel?

Some scholars, such as Umberto Cassuto, argue that God placed the Sabbath command in the Decalogue to remind the Israelites that he is the creator of the world. Cassuto states that 'were it not for this underlying thought, which links the sabbath to a basic idea in the relationship between the children of Israel and God, this commandment would have no place here.'[5] He goes on to argue that the Sabbath, even in Genesis 2:3, functioned merely as the antithesis to Mesopotamian religious beliefs.[6] While Genesis 2:3 is certainly antithetical to the beliefs of the ancient Near East and therefore carries a polemic function, nevertheless simply to identify the fourth commandment as a memorial to the creation fails to take into consideration the forward-looking, or eschatological, nature of the Sabbath. The Sabbath's eschatological nature is elaborated most clearly in the epistle to the Hebrews, where the third and fourth chapters provide divine commentary regarding the protological Sabbath and its relationship to Israel. In these two chapters the author of Hebrews comments on Numbers 14, Psalm 95:11, and Genesis 2:2, explaining the relationship of the Sabbath to Israel, Christ, and the Church.

---

[5]Umberto Cassuto, *A Commentary on the Book of Exodus* (1967; Jerusalem: Magnes Press, 1997), p. 244. Along these lines rabbinic interpretation sees the connection between Sabbath and protology, but the link is ultimately not to creation but to the Torah. According to rabbinic interpretation, some scholars argue that the Torah was created 2,000 years before the world and therefore has precedent over the creation (see *Mid. Rabb.* Gen. 1.1, 4).

[6]Cassuto, *Exodus*, pp. 65ff.

In Hebrews 4:1 the author makes clear that there is a promise to enter the rest of God. Of what rest does the author speak? He speaks of God's rest on the seventh day of the creation week: 'For he has somewhere spoken of the seventh day in this way: "And God rested on the seventh day from all his works" ' (Heb. 4:4; cf. Gen. 2:2). The author draws the connection of the rest of the seventh day and the Israelites by quoting Psalm 95:11: 'For we who have believed enter that rest, as he has said, "As I swore in my wrath, 'They shall not enter my rest,' " although his works were finished from the foundation of the world' (Heb. 4:3). The author makes the point that Israel failed to enter the seventh day of the creation week when they were on the verge of entering the promised land. The promised land itself was not the rest of which Psalm 95 speaks, the author writing that, 'For if Joshua had given them rest, God would not have spoken of another day later on' (Heb. 4:8). The rest was not a temporal resting in the promised land. Rather, it is God's rest subsequent to his creation labor as he took up residence in the temple of the archetypal heavens on the eternal seventh day.[7] The promised land serves as a type of heaven, the locale of God's seventh day rest.[8] What is it that separates those who enter God's rest from those who do not enter it? Faith. 'For indeed the gospel was preached to us as well as to them; but the word which they heard did not profit them, not being

---

[7] Meredith G. Kline, *The Structure of Biblical Authority* (1989; Eugene: Wipf & Stock, 1997), p. 87.

[8] Geerhardus Vos, *The Teaching of the Epistle to the Hebrews* (Eugene: Wipf & Stock, 1998), p. 66; Jon Laansma, *I Will Give You Rest* (Tübingen: Mohr Siebeck, 1997), pp. 282, 352; William L. Lane, *Hebrews 1-8*, WBC, vol. 47a (Dallas: Word, 1991), p. 99; cf. A. T. Lincoln, 'Sabbath, Rest, and Eschatology in the New Testament,' in *From Sabbath to Lord's Day*, ed. D. A. Carson (Eugene: Wipf & Stock, 1999), pp. 208-09; contra Rushdoony who argues that the Sabbath command points to a 'second creation rest.' The rest of God began at the creation and continues; it does not terminate and start anew (Rousas John Rushdoony, *Institutes of Biblical Law* [Nutley: P & R, 1973], p. 143).

mixed with faith in those who heard it' (Heb. 4:2; NKJV). [9] A summary of the data collected thus far is in order.

Israel, as God's son, was placed at the edge of the promised land, a type of the eternal rest of the seventh day, but because of the people's lack of faith they did not enter the Sabbath rest of God. This shows that the Sabbath rest of the seventh day is incorporated in the Decalogue, not simply as a reminder that God is the creator, but that he is also the eschatological Lord.[10] The Sabbath serves as an eschatological sign to the people of Israel, a portion of time that points forward to the eschatological rest of God. This sign aspect of the Sabbath is brought out in Exodus 31:17, where God tells his people that the Sabbath is 'a sign forever between me and the people of Israel that in six days the LORD made heaven and earth, and on the seventh day he rested and was refreshed.' Just as God concluded the creation of the first Adam and the garden-temple by giving the Sabbath, upon the completion of the tabernacle and the creation of Israel, his son and type of the second Adam, God gives the Israelites the sign of the Sabbath. Peter Enns explains that

> it is most fitting that the Sabbath be the sign of this covenant. Israel, as we have noted, is a new creation. This is a new people of God, whom he intends to use to undo the work of the first man. Also, the tabernacle is a microcosm of the created order, a parcel of edenic splendor established amid the chaos of the world. The Sabbath is not just a reminder of the original creation in Genesis 1 and 2, but a reminder of God's re-creation of the cosmos in the tabernacle.[11]

---

[9]Richard B. Gaffin, 'A Sabbath Rest Still Awaits the People of God,' in *Pressing Toward the Mark*, ed. Charles G. Dennison & Richard C. Gamble (Philadelphia: The Committee for the Historian of the OPC, 1986), pp. 38-39.

[10]Laansma, *Rest*, p. 295.

[11]Peter Enns, *Exodus*, NIVAC (Grand Rapids: Zondervan, 2000), pp. 544-45; cf. Brevard S. Childs, *The Book of Exodus*, OTL (1974;

Once again, the Sabbath, an eschatological sign, is brought in from the realm of protology. One must take note, however, that after the fall the Sabbath now also functions as a soteriological sign.

God instructs Moses to tell the Israelites that, 'Above all you shall keep my Sabbaths, for this is a sign between me and you throughout your generations, that you may know that I, the LORD, sanctify you' (Exod. 31:13). One must remember that the specter of sin looms and the basis of Israel's entrance into the eschatological rest of God is promise and grace, not their labor. It is only through the work of the second Adam that Israel would be able ultimately to enter the rest of the seventh day, which is represented by the sign of the weekly recurring Sabbath (Heb. 9:15). Most likely, it is for this reason that any attempt to labor on the Sabbath, which was the sign of God working on their behalf and sanctifying them and the eschatological goal of creation, was met with the penalty of death (Exod. 31:14-15). Entrance to the seventh day rest of the creation week at this point in redemptive history was on the basis of promise and gospel, not by works. The Sabbath, under the Mosaic economy, is a visual and typological picture of Paul's statement, 'For the wages of sin is death, but the free gift of God is eternal life in Christ Jesus our Lord' (Rom. 6:23).[12] The connection between the Sabbath and Romans 6:23 will be dealt with in greater detail below.

Louisville: Westminster, 1976), p. 542; John I. Durham, *Exodus*, WBC, vol. 3 (Dallas: Word, 1987), pp. 413-14; also Laansma, *Rest*, p. 69.

[12]See the general comments of John Murray, *The Epistle to the Romans*, NICNT (Grand Rapids: Eerdmans, 1968), pp. 237-38; Douglas Moo, *The Epistle to the Romans*, NICNT (Grand Rapids: Eerdmans, 1996), p. 408. Contra Rushdoony, who argues that Israel was given the dominion mandate, not as a typological forerunner, but as something they could actually carry out: 'The redeemed man's work is not an attempt to *create* a paradise on earth, but to *fulfill* God's requirements within the kingdom. The redeemed man is a citizen of the Kingdom of God, and he abides by the laws thereof: this

For now, one may summarize that the Sabbath still serves as an eschatological sign of God's seventh day rest of Genesis 2:2. The original rest of the creation into which Adam was to enter still stands as the eschatological goal. Adam did not enter that eschatological rest, which was once again presented to Israel, God's son, who was placed in an edenic paradise and who was to fulfill the broken covenant of works. Yet, Israel could not fulfill the broken covenant because of the presence of sin. This means that, on the level of the *ordo salutis*, the Israelite enters the eternal eschatological rest of the seventh day by grace through faith in Christ. Israel is under the covenant of grace, not the covenant of works. On the level of the *historia salutis*, Israel serves as a type that points forward to the person and work of the second Adam.[13] What about the relationship between Christ and the Sabbath?

The second Adam and the Sabbath

Concerning the relationship between Christ and the Sabbath, one must return to the fourth chapter of Hebrews. As previously stated, Israel, God's son and type of the second Adam, did not enter the eternal Sabbath rest. The author of Hebrews states, however, that Christ has entered the rest of the seventh day (Heb. 10:12-13). He has entered the archetypal temple where God began his rest on the seventh day. Unlike Adam, who did not enter the eschatological rest, Christ, the second Adam, did accomplish the work and has rested from his labors. There are two points that must be addressed in connection with the second Adam and entering the Sabbath rest of God, namely, inaugurated and consummated eschatology.

---

is his work, his duty, and his path to dominion. The fact of the sabbath presupposes the fact of work' (Rushdoony, *Biblical Law*, p. 147).

[13]C. K. Barrett, 'The Eschatology of the Epistle to the Hebrews,' in *The Background of the New Testament and Its Eschatology*, eds. W. D. Davies and D. Daube (Cambridge: Cambridge University Press, 1956), pp. 367-68.

First, there is an aspect to the work of the second Adam that has already been accomplished. Richard Gaffin writes that

> the way in which Psalm 95 and Genesis 2 are brought together here indicates the scope of the promised rest in the writer's view. The fulfillment of the church's hope represents nothing less than the fulfillment of the original purpose of God in creation, or more accurately, the realization of his purposes of redemption is the means to the end of realizing his purposes of creation.[14]

The inaugurated eschatological aspect of the work of Christ is in his entering the Sabbath rest of creation. In this regard the Apostle Paul quotes Psalm 8:6: 'For "God has put all things in subjection under his feet," ' in connection with the resurrection of Christ (1 Cor. 15:27; Heb. 2:7-8). Christ, as the head of the body, has inaugurated the new creation with his own resurrection from the dead on the first day of the week, just as the first creation began on Sunday.[15] The inauguration of the new creation has begun, but one must not think that it has been consummated.[16] The new creation's inauguration is seen quite clearly when Christ quotes Isaiah 61:1-2 at the beginning of his ministry:

> The Spirit of the Lord is upon me, because he has anointed me to proclaim good news to the poor. He has sent me to proclaim liberty to the captives and recovering of sight to the blind, to set at liberty those who are oppressed, to proclaim the year of the Lord's favor (Luke 4:18-19).

---

[14]Gaffin, 'A Sabbath Rest,' p. 40.
[15]Wright, *Resurrection*, p. 440; see also similarly Karl Barth, *Church Dogmatics*, vol. 3.1, *The Doctrine of Creation*, trans. J. W. Edwards, et al. (1958; Edinburgh: T & T Clark, 1998), pp. 224ff.
[16]Laansma, *Rest*, p. 307.

What is significant about Christ reading this passage and making the claim, 'Today this Scripture has been fulfilled in your hearing' (Luke 4:21), is that the text is connected to the year of Jubilee (Lev. 25:8-17), which is the culmination of seven seven-year sabbaticals.[17] Since the year of Jubilee is based in the eschatological seventh day rest of God, Christ is saying that the eschatological age has dawned with his own ministry.[18]

Second, there is an aspect to the work of the second Adam that has yet to come or be consummated, this aspect being plainly illustrated in the structure of Hebrews 3 and 4. Gaffin rightly argues that the passage is marked by triumph and testing. The 'present time is defined both by the eschatological triumph of Christ, their high priest in heaven, and the severe testing of the church. These two factors are always kept together; the one is never allowed to tone down or eclipse the other.'[19] This statement helps one to understand the nature of the completed work of Christ as it relates to its temporal manifestation. The new creation has begun, but it will not be consummated until the second advent of Christ (Rev. 21–22). Only then will one see the completed work of the second Adam in its fullness.[20] This evidence presents the investigator with important information regarding the Sabbath or, as it is now known, the Lord's Day (Rev. 1:10; cf. Acts 20:7; 1 Cor. 16:2).

The Lord's Day, or Sunday, is still rooted in protology, as is clear from the connection between Genesis 2:2,

---

[17]Darrell L. Bock, *Luke 1.1-9.50*, BECNT (Grand Rapids: Baker, 1994), p. 408; John E. Hartley, *Leviticus*, WBC, vol. 4 (Dallas: Word, 1992), pp. 446-47; Brevard S. Childs, *Biblical Theology of the Old and New Testaments* (Minneapolis: Fortress, 1992), p. 401.

[18]E. J. Young, *The Book of Isaiah*, vol. 3 (1972; Grand Rapids: Eerdmans, 1997), p. 460; cf. Vos, *Hebrews*, p. 55; and Meredith G. Kline, 'The Covenant of the Seventieth Week,' in *The Law and the Prophets*, ed. John H. Skilton (Nutley: P & R, 1974), p. 460.

[19]Gaffin, 'A Sabbath Rest,' pp. 35-36; also Barrett, 'Eschatology of Hebrews,' p. 372.

[20]Barrett, 'Eschatology of Hebrews,' p. 391.

Psalm 95:11, and the life, death, and resurrection of Christ. The people of God do not, however, labor for six days and then rest, as would have Adam, with the Sabbath as a sign of the yet-to-come eschaton and the completion of his work, or in the case of Israel, who served as a type of the second Adam and his work. The pattern in the Old Testament is first work, then rest. The New Testament pattern, in the light of the fulfillment of the Old Testament types of Adam and Israel, is one of first rest, then work. The idea is that the second Adam has completed the work on behalf of the people of God and the Church now rests each and every Lord's Day by commemorating the completion of that work – which was the entrance of the second Adam into the eschatological rest of the seventh day – and the inauguration of the new creation as she anticipates its consummation at the end of the present evil age (Gal. 1:4).[21] Vos writes:

> Inasmuch as the Old Covenant was still looking forward to the performance of the Messianic work, naturally the days of labor to it come first, the day of rest falls at the end of the week. We, under the New Covenant, look back upon the accomplished work of Christ. We, therefore, first celebrate the rest in principle procured by Christ, although the Sabbath also still remains a sign looking forward to the final eschatological rest.[22]

So too Gaffin comments that 'although the writer does not say so explicitly, the clear implication is that recurring Sabbath observance has its significance as a

---

[21]Gaffin, 'A Sabbath Rest,' p. 51, n. 37.

[22]Vos, *Biblical Theology*, p. 141. Wolfhart Pannenberg draws attention to the Jewish expectation of a completion of the seventh day of creation and the beginning of an 'eighth day of creation, which as the first day of a new week corresponds to the first day of creation in its function as a new beginning' (see 4 Esd. 7.29-31) (Wolfhart Pannenberg, *Systematic Theology*, vol. 2, trans. Geoffrey W. Bromiley [Grand Rapids: Eerdmans, 1991], pp. 144-45); so also Barrett, 'Eschatology of Hebrews,' p. 370.

sign or type of eschatological rest.'[23] The Lord's Day, or Sunday, then, protects 'against tendencies to blur or even lose sight of the difference between the eschatological "already" and "not yet".'[24] This tension between inaugurated and consummated eschatological Sabbath appears in three places, in Hebrews 4, Romans 6, and 1 Corinthians 15.

In connection to the eschatological rest of the seventh day, the author of Hebrews writes, 'For we who have believed enter that rest' (Heb. 4:3). But entering that rest upon regeneration does not mean that the believer enters the seventh day rest of God *in toto*. That regeneration is not a complete entrance to the seventh day rest is quite clear when the author of Hebrews states that 'there remains a Sabbath rest for the people of God' (Heb. 4:9). Paul draws this point out in Romans 6 when he writes that, 'We were buried therefore with him by baptism into death, in order that, just as Christ was raised from the dead by the glory of the Father, we too might walk in newness of life' (Rom. 6:4). Given the protological connections to baptism, namely, the waters of Genesis 1:2, 9 and the creation that emerges from them and baptism as the waters of the new creation, one can see that the regenerate are brought out from under the aegis of the first Adam and the old creation and brought under the aegis of the second Adam and the new creation. Or, in other words, baptism visually symbolizes emerging into the new creation, or the eschatological Sabbath rest of God. This theme is coupled to Romans 5:12-19.

Recall the typological repetition of the creation emerging with the Holy Spirit hovering over the waters (Gen. 1:2, 9), the creation re-emerging from the deluge with the dove flying over the waters (Gen. 8:10-11), Israel emerging from the water of the Red Sea accompanied by

---

[23]Gaffin, 'A Sabbath Rest,' p. 41.
[24]Gaffin, 'A Sabbath Rest,' p. 49.

the Holy Spirit described in avian terms (Deut. 32:11; Exod. 13; Hag. 2:5; Isa. 63:11), and the antitypical fulfillment with Christ the second Adam emerging from the water with the Holy Spirit present in the form of a dove (Luke 3:21-22). Protology informs the subsequent typology of the Old Testament and then finds its fulfillment in the antitype, Christ and his work. It is this matrix of protological typology that informs Romans 5 and 6 and particularly the idea of baptism into Christ. Just as the Israelites emerged from the waters of the Red Sea accompanied by the Holy Spirit, so too the Church emerges from the waters of baptism raised to walk in the newness of life by the power of the Holy Spirit (Rom. 6:4; 8:1ff; cf. 1 Pet. 3:20-21). Subsequent to passing through the Red Sea, a baptism (1 Cor. 10:2), Israel received the Law and the Sabbath command, violation of the latter bringing death. Why?

The Sabbath pointed forward to the work of Christ and the idea was that the Israelites would enter the seventh day rest by grace through the work of another, and not by their own works. If they labored on the Sabbath, it was a declaration that they themselves could secure the Sabbath rest by their own efforts. After the entrance of sin, the only thing that man's labor merits him is death, hence the severe penalty for violating the Sabbath. In this regard N. T. Wright notes that in Romans 6 Paul

> has explored the meaning of 5:12-21 in terms of the human renewal that results from the 'new exodus' of baptism. ... His concern has been to emphasize that when Christians look at the Adam / Christ contrast they should be in no doubt that they belong to the Christ side of it. This must, of course, be put into effect by the moral effort of not letting sin reign in the 'mortal body'; but this ongoing struggle is not to be thought of in terms of the Christian being some kind of a hybrid, half in Adam and half in Christ. The theology of baptism, both in terms of the 'new exodus' and in terms of the dying and rising of the Messiah, prohibits such a thing.

That which has happened has happened once for all. ... At the heart of it stands the sending, the death and the resurrection of the Messiah, God's son, to take on himself the weight of Adamic and Torah-driven trespass, and then to welcome into new life those who through suffering and prayer are led by the Spirit towards the promised inheritance. This is where we see at last what 'the obedience of the Messiah,' the theological driving heart of 5:12-21, really meant.[25]

It should be no surprise that after Paul explains the significance of baptism – the new exodus, the emergence of the new creation – he concludes with the words: 'For the wages of sin is death, but the free gift of God is eternal life in Christ Jesus our Lord' (Rom. 6:23). The relationship between the death penalty connected to the Sabbath command under the Mosaic covenant and the wages of sin in Romans 6:23 is one of type and antitype, namely temporal and eternal death (Heb. 2:1-4).[26] The New Testament believer, just as the Old Testament believer, is reminded on the heels of the new exodus that salvation is by the work of another, the second Adam, and that entrance to the promised land, or heaven, cannot be merited. The only thing that can be merited by the works of sinful man is death.

The Sabbath, rooted in protology, stands in a direct relationship to the Sabbath of Israel and its fulfillment in the work of the second Adam in the Lord's Day. Though the second Adam has been raised to rule in dominion over the earth, which is a manifestation of realized eschatology, the people of God still pilgrim to the heavenly city; the events of consummated eschatology lie in the future. Just as the Sabbath

---

[25]N. T. Wright, *Romans*, NIB (Nashville: Abingdon, 2002), pp. 546-47.

[26]See Leonhard Goppelt, *Typos*, trans. Donald H. Madvig (Grand Rapids: Eerdmans, 1982), pp. 172-73; Lane, *Hebrews*, pp. 37-38; Vos, *Biblical Theology*, p. 127.

pointed to the protological rest of God and the need for the Israelites to enter that rest, so too the Lord's Day points to the same rest. The difference lies in that the work of the second Adam has been accomplished and fulfilled, and the new creation has begun; hence the Lord's Day is on the first day of the week rather than the last. The Sabbath, though rooted in protology, has imbedded in it the eschatological principle, which has significant implications for the proper understanding of the relationship between eschatology and the rest of the doctrinal loci of systematic theology. It is to this relationship that one must now turn.

Eschatology and the other doctrinal loci

Eschatology is rooted in protology, its ultimate conclusion being revealed in pre-redemptive history and therefore preceding soteriology. A cursory examination of a cross-section of systematic theologies reveals that eschatology is often treated at the end of the system as something akin to an appendix. The usual result of this type of structure is that people believe that eschatology deals only with the days immediately preceding the return of Christ. This, however, is a misunderstanding of the nature of eschatology. As Vos notes, 'the eschatological principle is so deeply embedded in the structure of biblical religion as to precede and underlie everything else.'[27] This is so because eschatology, in terms of the Sabbath rest of the seventh day, is present in the beginning of the creation. When Adam fell, he forfeited his ability to enter God's rest of the seventh day by his own merit, setting redemptive history in motion that culminated in the advent of the second Adam and the inauguration of the new creation. In this connection one should note several items of importance as they specifically relate to the primacy of protology and eschatology over soteriology.

---

[27]Vos, *Pauline Eschatology*, p. 66.

First, 'the eschatological process is intended not only to put man back at the point where he stood before the invasion of sin and death, but to carry him higher to a plane of life, not attained before the probation, nor, so far as we can see, attainable without it.'[28] This is evident by contrasting that Adam stood in the garden-temple naked (Gen. 2:25) with the reality that the new Adamic humanity will stand in the eschatological temple clothed in the righteousness of Christ (Rom. 3:21-22; 5:17; cf. Rev. 7:9-14). Moreover, 'the eschatological state is before all else a state in which the enjoyment of Jehovah, the beatific vision of his face, the pleasures at his right hand, the perpetual dwelling with him in his sanctuary, form the supreme good.'[29] This supreme good, however, is one that is immutable, the *non posse peccare et mori*, an indefectible state, unlike the mutable state of Adam in the garden-temple, the *posse peccare et mori*. As Vos notes,

> If Christ placed us back there where Adam stood in his rectitude, without sins and without death, this would be unspeakable grace indeed, more than enough to make the gospel a blessed word. But grace exceeds sin far more abundantly than all this: besides wiping out the last vestige of sin and its consequences, it opens up for us that higher world to whose threshold even the first Adam had not yet apprehended. And this is not a mere matter of degrees in blessedness, it is a difference between two modes of life; as heaven is high above the earth, by so much the conditions of our future state will transcend those of the paradise of old.[30]

---

[28]Vos, *Pauline Eschatology*, p. 72.

[29]Vos, *Pauline Eschatology*, p. 349; also Jürgen Moltmann, *Theology of Hope* (1965; New York: Harper & Row, 1975), pp. 115-30; Childs, *Biblical Theology*, p. 392.

[30]Geerhardus Vos, *Grace and Glory* (1922; Edinburgh: Banner of Truth, 1994), p. 166.

Hence, mankind does not return to the garden but advances to a higher plane in the eschaton, an estate that bears many of the characteristics of the beginning.

Second, there is another implication of the primacy of protology and eschatology in that all of soteriology is an eschatological event. The fall of Adam set the stage for the necessity of the second Adam. Or, one may divide history into the epochs of the protological and eschatological Adams. There is, however, no clean line of division between the two epochs; it is not that the old creation ends and the new creation begins. Rather, the old and new creations overlap.[31] With the work of the second Adam, the new creation is inaugurated in the middle of the old creation. The following diagram illustrates the common understanding in contrast to the biblical model:[32]

Common Scheme

Already-Not-yet

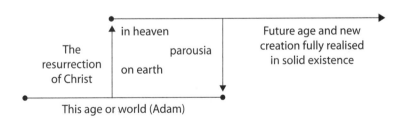

---

[31]Thomas R. Schreiner, *Paul Apostle of God's Glory in Christ* (Downers Grove: InterVarsity Press, 2001), p. 143.

Soteriology is the work of the second Adam and the Holy Spirit, the power of the eschatological age to come (Heb. 6:4). Consequently the entirety of soteriology is an eschatological manifestation of the power of the age to come.[33] In this regard, Jürgen Moltmann correctly observes that

> from first to last, and not merely in the epilogue, Christianity is eschatology, is hope, forward looking and forward moving, and therefore also revolutionizing and transforming the present. The eschatological is not one element of Christianity, but is the medium of the Christian faith as such, the key in which everything is set. ... Hence eschatology cannot really be only a part of Christian doctrine. Rather, the eschatological outlook is characteristic of all Christian proclamation, and of every Christian existence and of the whole church.[34]

Eschatology, therefore, is not merely the final locus at the end of systematic theology. Rather, it is the lens through which all other loci must be understood.[35]

Third, the hermeneutical priority of eschatology means that contrary to many of the current approaches to the study of Genesis 1–3, understanding the beginning of the Scriptures cannot be divorced from the end.[36] Many commentaries and monographs, especially those inter-

---

[32]This diagram is adapted from Vos, *Pauline Eschatology*, p. 38, n. 45.

[33]Vos, *Pauline Eschatology*, pp. 37-38; idem, *Hebrews*, p. 50.

[34]Moltmann, *Theology of Hope*, p. 16; cf. Childs, *Biblical Theology*, p. 395.

[35]Michael S. Horton, *Covenant and Eschatology* (Louisville: Westminster/John Knox, 2002), p. 5; also N. A. Dahl, 'Christ, Creation and the Church,' in *The Background of the New Testament and Its Eschatology*, eds. W. D. Davies and D. Daube (Cambridge: Cambridge University Press, 1956), p. 423.

[36]The Qumran community had an appreciation for the principle that the end gives an understanding of the beginning: 'You will understand the end of the ages and you will gaze at ancient things to know' (4 Q 298 frs. 3-4ii).

ested in science, make little or no reference to the second Adam and see the purpose of Genesis as primarily scientific. Hugh Ross, for example, writes that, 'In the case of Genesis 1–11 the content is largely scientific (as well as historical and spiritual, of course).'[37] But Genesis 1–3 was not intended to be read as a document detailing the scientific origins of the cosmos.[38] The reason for Genesis 1–3 was not to refute Charles Darwin and scientific evolutionary theory. On the contrary, it was intended to show the work of the first Adam, which is foundational to comprehending properly the work of the second Adam. A clear picture of the results of the work of the second Adam appears in the eschatological imagery in Scripture. Therefore, the analogy of Scripture, especially as it relates to christology and eschatology, and not science, provides the reader with the interpretive key for Genesis 1–3, or protology. In this vein Wolfhart Pannenberg writes

If the eschatological future of God in the coming of his kingdom is the standpoint from which to understand the world as a whole, the view of its beginning cannot be unaffected. This beginning loses its function as an unalterably valid basis of unity in the whole process. It is now merely the beginning of that which will achieve its full form and true individuality only at the end. Only in the light of the eschatological consummation can we of the world understand the meaning of its beginning. ... This comes to expression in the primitive Christian proclamation that we must believe in Jesus Christ as

---

[37]Hugh Ross, *The Genesis Question* (Colorado Springs: Navpress, 2001), pp. 7-8.

[38]Childs comments that conflict between the Enlightenment and the doctrine of creation 'had been long sown within Christian theology by shifting the theological focus of creation to issues of origins and causality. By defining creation primarily in terms of unrepeatable origins, Protestant theology made the Deist attack and its own defense more difficult. ... Certainly the controversy with the Deists and Cartesians contributed to the church's incapacity to cope with Darwin and his predecessors' (Childs, *Biblical Theology*, p. 403).

the mediator of creation as well as the eschatological bringer of salvation. From the standpoint of Christian typology all that preceded the earthly appearance of Jesus is thus a shadowy prefiguration of the truth that came to light in him. But can we reconcile this view of the relation between eschatology and creation with the scientific description of the universe?[39]

Protology is not about science; it is ultimately about the second Adam. Genesis 1–3 is no more about science than is Paul's epistle to the Romans. One does not turn to Romans for science and likewise one should not turn to Genesis for science.

The three points above demonstrate the importance of the primacy of protology and eschatology with the rest of the loci of systematic theology. By understanding the relationship of the protological Sabbath to eschatology, and its logical and chronological precedence over soteriology, one is provided not simply with the end of the story but rather the lens through which the whole story must be read.[40]

Conclusion

Throughout this survey of the nature of the seventh day of God's creation week the investigation has demonstrated

---

[39]Pannenberg, *Systematic Theology*, p. 146; similarly Childs, *Biblical Theology*, pp. 385-86, 405.

[40]Dahl, 'Christ, Creation, and Church,' p. 424. This not a novel way to read Genesis 1–3, nor is it unique to make the connections between protology, christology, and eschatology. The *Epistle of Barnabas* (c. AD 100) states: 'For the Scripture says concerning us, while He speaks to the Son, "Let us make man after Our image, and after Our likeness; and let them have dominion over the beasts of the earth, and the fowls of heaven, and the fishes of the sea." And the Lord said, on beholding the fair creature man, "Increase, and multiply, and replenish the earth." These things were spoken to the Son. Again, I will show thee how, in respect to us, He has accomplished a second fashioning in these last days' (*ANF*, vol. 1, § 6.13, pp. 140-41). Notice how the author connects Genesis 1:26-28 with christology and eschatology.

how that day served as an eschatological sign to Adam of the covenant of works. The study has also shown how it was related to Israel as a sign of the Mosaic covenant – a sign that God was working in the midst of Israel, that their labor would not secure the eschatological rest, and that there was a terminus to Israel's covenantal labors. The Sabbath and Israel typified the work of the second Adam. The second Adam successfully fulfilled the obligations of the broken covenant of works and entered the seventh day rest of God and for this reason the Church no longer rests on the last day of the week. Christ inaugurated the eschatological age, the new creation, which started with his resurrection from the dead on Sunday, the first day of the week. This is why the Church observes its day of rest on Sunday. The Lord's Day still serves as an eschatological sign of the covenant, a sign that points to the future consummation of the new creation. The Sabbath of protology, which is the eschatological principle, also has important implications for one's comprehension of the relationship of eschatology to the rest of systematic theology – eschatology is the interpretive lens through which one must understand the whole. With the conclusion of the study of the major themes of protology and their connections to the rest of the loci of systematic theology, some general observations and concluding remarks are in order.

7

Conclusion

This essay began with the claim that there was a way to cut through the current debate surrounding the interpretation of Genesis 1–3. Rather than looking at Genesis 1–3 through the lens of science or narrowing the focus to determining the length of the days of creation, the study examined by means of the *analogia fidei* (the immediate historical context within which Genesis was written and the three chapters' ultimate christological and eschatological significance). These interpretive principles have helped move towards correctly interpreting Genesis 1–3. The opening chapters of the Bible are not about science, rather they find their meaning and significance in the light of the second Adam, Jesus Christ.

Too often, interpreters fragment Genesis 1–3, either by supposing that it is made up of multiple sources, such as the documentary hypothesis, or reading it exclusively through an ontological and systematic theological lens. When Genesis 1–3 is read against the backdrop of redemptive history and within the context of the relationship between the first and second Adams, a clear and coherent picture emerges. This method of reading Genesis is nothing more than using the New Testament to interpret the Old.

When Genesis is interpreted in the light of Jesus Christ, a clearer picture of the relationship between the first and second Adams emerges. There are those who misuse Genesis for scientific purposes with the hopes of convincing doubters of the scientific validity of the teaching of Scripture. Others place their efforts on the interpretation of the length of the days hoping the 24-hour paradigm alone will serve as a bulwark against Darwinian evolution and theological liberalism within the Church. Yet, despite these doubtless well-intended efforts, many miss the ultimate significance of Genesis 1–3. It is only Christ who can convince the unbeliever of the truth. Only the second Adam, by the power of the Holy Spirit, can bring a person out from under the power of sin and death, the world of the first Adam, and bring him under the aegis of the world of the second Adam.

Finally, several observations regarding the relationship between the loci of systematic theology have been made. Too many interpreters come to Genesis 1–3 interested only in questions of systematic theology or ontology, namely, the origins of man and the physical world. Little to no attention is given to the redemptive historic context of the creation. Moreover, few make the connections between protology, soteriology, christology, ecclesiology, and eschatology. Indeed, the end informs the beginning, and it is the beginning that informs the activity of the second Adam both in his own person and work as well as the redemption of the people of God. Protology does not drift away after leaving Genesis 1–3 but is instead embossed across all of redemptive history. God does not amend the vocation of the first Adam but instead sends One who will obediently fulfill his calling.

Genesis 1–3 must be read holistically, in the light of the revelation of Jesus Christ, the second Adam. To divorce Genesis 1–3 from Christ is to do violence to the whole of Scripture. Rather than searching for molecules and atoms in the pages of Scripture, should one not be in search of the two Adams? One must follow Christ as he interpreted the Old Testament Scriptures on the road to Emmaus: 'And beginning with Moses and all the

Prophets, he interpreted to them in all the Scriptures the things concerning himself' (Luke 24.27). May this essay be a step forward in reading Genesis 1–3, shadows of the second Adam, aright. The Church must read Genesis in the light of Christ and eschatology, the second and faithful Adam, the alpha and omega, the beginning and the end. In other words, one must read Genesis by considering last things first. *Soli Deo Gloria.*

Themes Index

209

Persons Index

Abel 27, 121
Abimelech 87
Abraham *see* Abrahamic covenant *in*
    index of themes
Adam *see index of themes*
Augustine of Hippo 92–3, 103

Barrett, C. K. 129n38
Barth, Karl 74, 100, 102
Bavinck, Herman 51, 53, 54–5, 91
Beale, G. K. 48–9, 125, 134,
    .... 135, 176, 179, 181–2

Berkhof, Louis 147–8
Blocher, Henri 27
Brakel, Wilhelmus à 90
Brunner, Emil 29–30
Bryan, William Jennings 18

Cain 27, 121
Calvin, John *see index of themes*
Cassuto, Umberto 42, 138n54, 186
Childs, Brevard S. 201n38
Copernicus, Nicholas 21
Cranfield, C. E. B. 92
Cullmann, Oscar 156

Dabney, R. L. 28–9
Darwin, Charles 14
David, King 133–6
    see also Davidic covenant *in index of*
    themes
Delitzsch, Franz 91, 100
Dumbrell, William 88, 133
Duncan, Ligon 22
Dunn, James 94, 123–4, 158n25,
    .... 166, 173
Duns Scotus, John 108n64
Durham, John I. 125–6

Einstein, Albert 21
Einwechter, William 170

Elijah 36
Ellis, E. Earle 149
Enns, Peter 188
Enoch 44
Erickson, Millard 43
Eve *see index of themes*

Gaffin, Richard 109n66, 166,
    .... 191, 193–4
Gage, Warren Austin 117–18, 131
Gentry, Kenneth 171
Gunkel, Herman 41, 44

Hall, David 22
Hodge, A. A. 91
Hodge, Charles 15, 16, 21, 93, 110
Hoekema, Anthony 45, 47, 52, 53, 54

Irons, Lee 107–8n64, 110
Isaac 122

Jacob 122
Jerome, St. 13
Jesus Christ *see index of themes*
Job 24–5
Josephus 70n29

Keil, C. F. 22, 41–2, 43, 100
Kelly, Douglas 17
Kidner, Derek 40n3
Kline, Meredith 41, 61, 73–4,
    .... 83–4, 109–10
Kraus, Hans-Joachim 136
Kuhn, Thomas 21
Kuyper, Abraham 21

Leupold, H. C. 22, 138, 151–2n12
Luther, Martin 13, 22, 43–4, 45,
    .... 57, 74, 90, 92

217

Scripture Index

Creation and Change

Genesis 1:1-2.4 in the Light of Changing Scientific Paradigms

Douglas F Kelly

"I greatly appreciate the content as well as the style of this book. It is the best work that I have read on this subject. The author's statements concerning the role of faith in science are very important; the subject is frequently misunderstood. With regard to this exegesis of the biblical text I hope that Douglas Kelly's courageous voice will be listened to."

Frederick N. Skiff, Professor of Physics,
University of Iowa

Douglas F. Kelly is Richard Jordan Professor at the Reformed Theological Seminary, Charlotte, North Carolina.

ISBN 1-85792-283-2

Rethinking Genesis

The Source and Authorship of the First Book of the Pentateuch

Duane Garrett

'Since its inception over a century ago the Documentary Theory of Pentateuchal origins has never gone unchallenged. It is the strength of Dr Garrett's study of Genesis that he goes beyond (mere) criticism of this extraordinarily resilient theory to the development of a credible and extremely illuminating, indeed, compelling alternative - one that is thoroughly biblical, impeccably scholarly and true to the pervasive Mosaism of the Pentateuchal books. This is a book deserving a wide readership and no reader will put it down unrewarded.'

Alec Motyer

Duane Garrett is John R. Sampey Professor of Old Testament at Southern Baptist Theological Seminary, Louisville, Kentucky.

ISBN 1-85792-576-9

Christian Focus Publications
publishes books for all ages

Our mission statement –

STAYING FAITHFUL
In dependence upon God we seek to help make His infallible Word, the Bible, relevant. Our aim is to ensure that the Lord Jesus Christ is presented as the only hope to obtain forgiveness of sin, live a useful life and look forward to heaven with Him.

REACHING OUT
Christ's last command requires us to reach out to our world with His gospel. We seek to help fulfill that by publishing books that point people towards Jesus and help them develop a Christ-like maturity. We aim to equip all levels of readers for life, work, ministry and mission.

Books in our adult range are published in three imprints.
   Christian Focus contains popular works including biographies, commentaries, basic doctrine and Christian living. Our children's books are also published in this imprint.
   Mentor focuses on books written at a level suitable for Bible College and seminary students, pastors, and other serious readers. The imprint includes commentaries, doctrinal studies, examination of current issues and church history.
   Christian Heritage contains classic writings from the past.

Christian Focus Publications, Ltd
Geanies House, Fearn, Ross-shire,
IV20 1TW, Scotland, United Kingdom
info@christianfocus.com

For details of our titles visit us on our website
www.christianfocus.com